PRIMARY

PROFESSIONAL

YOUNG
LITERACY
LEARNERS

how we can help them

MARGARET M CLARK

© 1994 Margaret M. Clark

Published by Scholastic Publications Ltd
Villiers House
Clarendon Avenue
Leamington Spa
Warwickshire CV32 5PR

Author Margaret M. Clark
Editor Juliet Gladston
Series Designer Lynne Joesbury
Designer Elizabeth Harrison

Designed using Aldus Pagemaker
Processed by Pages Bureau, Leamington Spa
Printed in Great Britain by Bell & Bain Ltd, Glasgow

The right of Margaret M. Clark to be identified as the Author
of this Work has been asserted by her in accordance with the
Copyright, Designs and Patents Act 1988

British Library Cataloguing-in-Publication Data
A catalogue record for this book is available from the British Library.

ISBN 0-590-53310-X

PRIMARY
PROFESSIONAL BOOKSHELF

CONTENTS

PRIMARY
PROFESSIONAL BOOKSHELF

PREFACE

Over the years I have written a number of books and articles for academic journals, mainly based on my researches. Even in such writing I have always tried to communicate with as wide a readership as possible. Last year I received an invitation from Gill Moore, editor of *Child Education*, to write a feature article on reading for the magazine. This was, for me, an exciting new venture. I was able to accept the challenge because I had recently spent some time in an inner city school, in a class of seven- and eight-year-olds, for many of whom English was not their first language. Thanks to these children and their teacher, I had been able to put into practice a number of my ideas which stimulated the children to produce a wide variety of written work, from which I could draw examples. I am grateful to Gill Moore of Scholastic for her faith in my ability to undertake such a different task. This book is a development from that article, and extension of the ideas outlined there. My thanks to Scholastic for commissioning me to write it and to the staff for all their support during its production. I would like in particular to thank Gina Nuttall, the Senior Commissioning Editor, and Juliet Gladston, Commissioning Editor, with whom I have worked most closely during the writing of the book. Their skilful editing has improved the language without distorting the message. Thanks also to Elizabeth Harrison, Designer, for translating the children's work into successful book illustrations.

In this book it has been possible to refer to only a minority of the authors whose work on the subject of literacy has influenced me; I hope those omitted on this occasion will forgive me. It did not seem appropriate here to give a history of the teaching of reading. Instead I chose for Chapter 1 to select a few key publications to act as signposts in tracing changes in our thinking about reading over the past twenty years. I am sure each reader will have their own particular authors they feel should have been included; however, few will dispute the importance of those I have chosen.

Many of the illustrations in the book have come from practical work in schools undertaken for their assignments or dissertations by students of mine; other examples have been selected from the wealth of material brought by teachers attending workshops I have conducted. I only regret that it is not possible to acknowledge everyone by name. Where a publication is available based on the work, I have noted that. For the rest I hope you all appreciate how grateful I am for all the fascinating examples I now possess, and can call upon for my writing and lectures. Most of the remaining examples are either from my own researches or my recent time in the inner city school. Many thanks to all the children whose drawings and writing I have included, and to the parents with whom I have had such interesting discussions. As I hope will become clear to readers, there is so much to be learned from looking at children's work and listening to their parents – and to the children themselves. Without all the practical examples this would have been a less readable book; it would also have given fewer insights into children as 'young literacy learners'.

I would also like to acknowledge William Murray for permission to reproduce the Key Words List; Falmer Press for permission to reproduce the illustration on page 50 from *New Directions in the Study of Reading,* edited by M.M.Clark (1985); Hodder & Stoughton for the sample prose in i.t.a. on page 75 from *Reading ¬ Which Approach?* by V. Southgate and G.R. Roberts (1970); the Controller of HMSO for the sample of diacritical marking on page 76 from the Plowden Report, *Children and their Primary Schools* (1967). The stories *One Up* and *When the Moon Winked* are reproduced by courtesy of Granada Television Ltd; GSN Educational Software was responsible for the computer analysis of the words in the stories for the television series.

Margaret M. Clark
April 1994

INTRODUCTION: SETTING THE SCENE

There was a time when many people assumed that reading was a skill acquired in the first few years in school; thereafter, it was believed that practice and their growing maturity would enable most children to read an increasingly varied number of texts without further specific instruction in reading. Now it is appreciated that important skills related to literacy have to be encouraged and supported throughout a child's school career, in primary and in secondary school. Only then will the children be enabled to read with understanding and enjoyment for a variety of purposes and communicate in writing in meaningful, interesting ways.

There was a time when parents were merely expected to send their children to school ready to learn to read and to accept and support the school in the instruction it provided. The extent of the parents' contribution tended to be measured in terms of the frequency of their visits to school, their acceptance of the school's advice and the numbers of books available in the home. The need for a partnership with parents is now more likely to be acknowledged. It is not too much of a caricature to suggest that the schools were given most of the credit for the children who succeeded; in contrast, the failures were often blamed on the parents, or the children themselves. Staff in pre-school units, likewise, were regarded as interfering were they seen to introduce anything which appeared to be instruction in reading and writing.

There was a time when the teaching of reading was regarded as the necessary foundation for the teaching of writing; thus facility in reading was expected to precede writing, at least of anything other than copying or tracing of writing composed by the teacher. There is now a greater tendency to regard the teaching of reading and writing as interrelated and to see each as potentially supporting the other from the earliest stages.

In contrast, was there ever a time when the standards of literacy were not a matter for concern, and thought to be falling? A search through the records clearly establishes this to be a perpetual cry over many years, with or without evidence to establish falling standards as a fact!

Most of the developments referred to above have taken place since I trained as a primary school teacher. My training involved lectures on the teaching of reading, where the points noted above were either explicit or implicit in the texts to which we were referred. Admittedly this was many years ago. Over the intervening years I have been involved in lecturing on literacy in many parts of the world. A number of the courses have been for teachers in training or experienced teachers undertaking postgraduate work. It has thus been possible for me to observe the changing emphases, and not least the strengths and weaknesses in these changes over the years. My lectures have, of course, necessitated that I keep up to date with the literature on reading. My interest in pre-school education was aroused by the request from an administrator, in the local authority in which I had been doing research on reading, that I undertake an assessment of their first nursery schools and make recommendations. The fact that I have continued to undertake research into pre-school education and to lecture on this topic, far from being a drawback and preventing me from a total commitment to the study of literacy, has increased my appreciation of the importance of the pre-school years and the contribution of the home to children's literacy development.

Early in my career I was for several years a primary school teacher, coping with a class of 54 seven- and eight-year-olds, with a very wide range of ability and varied levels of competence in reading and related skills. I had to meet this challenge at a time when, as now, resources were scarce and ingenuity crucial. On one occasion my headteacher expressed concern that he had heard loud laughter from my classroom; he wondered what we could have been doing! His concern was not that the class sounded unruly (he had heard the sounds through an open window as he taught in the next room). His concern appeared to be that he thought we must be wasting time; he felt I could not be concentrating on the 3Rs. His suspicions that I must be involved in something frivolous were not allayed when I explained that we were playing a game in which I tried to trick the children; on that particular occasion it happened to involve arithmetic! To him, learning was a serious business and couldn't be fun. He was all the more puzzled when he was given a good report of my work by the inspector, who claimed to be sufficiently impressed by my novel approaches that he asked to send a visitor to the school to observe in my classroom. I discovered many years later from someone who later became headteacher of that school and whom I met in another school in the course of my research, that this is recorded in the school log-book. Very recently, I was delighted to receive letters from children of a similar age in an inner city school with whom I had been working, in which they said how much they had enjoyed what we had been doing, mentioning specifically such things as the group work, making up spells, word puzzles, writing stories, even spelling. All the activities were planned to improve their competence in reading, writing and even spelling. I enjoyed myself as much as the children, which gives me justification for claiming that it can be fun for the adults as well as the children to learn in a supportive and yet challenging environment.

During my time as a primary school teacher I studied for a postgraduate degree in education on a part-time basis, which involved both lectures and empirical work for a dissertation. It was essential to undertake the empirical work in my own class as I would not have been released to do it elsewhere. In the event, this proved valuable as it helped to observe and analyse my own practice, given a framework within which to do so. The researches which I have undertaken over the past twenty-five years have all had to be carried out on a part-time basis; concurrently lecturing to students in training as educational psychologists, teachers in training or experienced teachers. Far from being a disadvantage, this has made it possible for me to bring alive for the students the dynamic nature of educational research. I, in return, have gained new insights from their comments and the practical examples they have included in their written work; these have included examples of children's work in different settings, both oral and written; discussions with the children themselves, with teachers and with parents on aspects of literacy. A number of the illustrations in this book have come from such assignments.

Over the past twenty-five years the research I have undertaken of relevance to reading has concerned:

✦ the characteristics of children in the primary school who have had prolonged difficulty in learning to read;

✦ children who were already reading when they entered school, their characteristics and those of their homes;

✦ studies of the literacy experiences of pre-school children in nursery schools and at home;

✦ an investigation into a school-based remedial service, undertaken at the request of the local authority, to make recommendations for its improvement;

✦ a study of pupils with learning difficulties in their first year in secondary school, to make recommendations as to how the schools' policies for such children could be improved.

I have thus been able to observe children and their teachers in many different settings, and talk with the parents of children who are succeeding and those who are perceived as failures. Hopefully, the insights I have gained from these sources will be reflected in this book. The aims of this book are:

✦ to outline the research evidence on which the changes referred to above are based;

✦ to analyse the ways in which our understanding of what is involved in becoming literate has been deepened;

✦ to explore the evidence from studies of young children in support of these changing views;

✦ to consider ways in which these insights can and should influence classroom practice.

In the following chapters each of these points is explored, illustrated where possible by the children themselves. I hope that you, the reader, will enjoy this book, and that if you do, you will not feel guilty. My aim, whether working with children, or with adults, has never been to try to teach or explain everything. I have hoped to be sensitive enough to their needs and misunderstandings to both support and challenge them. I have adopted a similar policy in writing this book. Rather than load the text with references, I have cited a selection of sources which have proved major influences in my thinking over the years. This I have backed with notes where appropriate at the end of chapters, and recommended reading from recent publications; within these you will find many further references should you need them. It has been possible to highlight in the text only a few of the insights which can be gained from careful observation of children's work, and in particular the examples I have included here. There are many other lessons which can be learned from studying them yourself. This I would encourage you to do, as a focus for discussion and to help you towards developing creative contexts to support and stimulate young children in their literacy learning in the classroom and in the home.

CHAPTER 1

NEW DIRECTIONS IN THE STUDY OF READING

SIGNPOSTS SINCE THE SEVENTIES

In the 1960s and early 1970s textbooks on reading tended to concentrate on:

✦ the initial teaching of reading within the first two years in school, with a great deal of space devoted to consideration of a possible best method of teaching reading;

✦ reading readiness measured in terms of tests of skills assumed to be associated with progress in reading;

✦ measurement of reading performance on short, simple standardised tests;

✦ contrasts in test performance between children who failed and children who succeeded;

✦ eye movements of good readers contrasted with eye movements of poor readers.

Surprisingly, in view of current statements by politicians and others, standards of reading were a matter of grave concern in the 1960s, with studies of backward readers, distress at the high incidence of adult illiterates and debate on the magnitude of the problem of dyslexia. Already in *A Language for Life* (DES 1975) (the report of the Bullock Committee established in 1969 because of concern at a claimed fall in reading standards in England), changes can be seen in official statements about literacy which reflect the findings of research. The importance of a 'whole school policy' for reading in both primary and secondary schools, the relationship between oral and written language and the complexity of the task of assessing reading progress are all issues considered in The Bullock Report. Its recommendations are developed further in The Kingman Report (DES 1988a) and in The Cox Report (DES 1988b) translated into a curriculum for reading, writing and listening, as a Core subject within the National Curriculum in England and Wales, with indications of ways in which children's progress can be assessed and monitored.

This book is not the place for a detailed history of reading research, extended consideration of the theoretical issues, or even a summary of research findings. There are many other sources for that information, to which reference will be made where appropriate in the following chapters. However, it seems important to draw attention to a few key books and studies which at the time of their publication presented controversial or unexpected views, views which came to be referred to in many subsequent publications on reading, which led to changes in emphasis in research and have influenced our thinking on literacy. I have selected for mention in this chapter seven such books to set the scene, in particular studies which have influenced the views expressed in this book.

UNDERSTANDING READING

In 1971 when the first edition of Frank Smith's book, *Understanding Reading*, was published it challenged many of the ideas about reading then current among teachers, and raised awareness of issues that had not been considered previously. Perhaps because Frank Smith had not himself come from the teaching profession, but had initially been a journalist before studying psychology, he was able to look with fresh eyes at many previously unquestioned 'facts' about reading. It was he who stressed the importance of appreciating the range and complexity of the skills brought to the reading situation by young children, and of building on these. The child needs to understand what are the *distinctive features of written language*. What is crucial if a child is to discover the critical similarities and differences between letters and between words 'is not so much a matter of knowing how to look as knowing what to look for' (Smith 1971, page 1). For this to take place the child must be provided with evidence, rather than instructions. That evidence should be such as to help the child to appreciate which letters or words are to be treated as 'the same' (irrespective of size or colour or style), and which as different for the purposes of reading. To show a child the letter 'h' repeatedly, saying it is 'h' because of its line at the side will not help the child to discriminate the letter. The presentation of 'h' and 'n' and of other letters in pairs and groups, together with feedback, which indicates that they are not to be treated as equivalent for the purposes of reading, is the kind of experience the child needs to discriminate letters from each other. Frank Smith also stresses the importance for a child of gaining knowledge of the way letters are grouped into words, which he refers to as 'orthographic information'. With such awareness, identification of the first letter of a word then helps you to predict the next letter. He quotes as an example the fact that in English, if the first letter of a word is 't' then the next letter is likely to be either 'h' or 'r' or a vowel.

Contrary to the belief of some people, Frank Smith does discuss phonics which he refers to as:

> ...a strategy for *mediated word identification* – a system for finding out the sound and meaning of a word that we cannot identify immediately, without asking someone else. (Smith 1971, page 160)

He is, however, critical of the place of 'phonics rules', many of which, as he points out, have so many exceptions that the child who attempts to apply them is likely to be unconvinced that such a system works! He places greater emphasis than others previously on the importance for the child of experience of reading; that we learn to read by reading, which will inevitably include making mistakes. He draws attention to the dangers of excessively slow reading even were it to be error free, since even good readers, in such circumstances, would lose the meaning of the passage. Although he states that much of the knowledge required for fluent reading 'cannot be taught', he does go on to state that 'the major contributions that the teacher can make are to provide information, feedback and encouragement' (Smith 1971, page 209).

Frank Smith still remains a controversial figure. While accepting that some of the statements he made in the 1970s are now being challenged by more recent research, such as his comments on the eye movements of skilled readers, we must not lose sight of the new horizons which he opened up. Indeed, many of his insights are as valid today as they were then.

READING: THE PATTERNING OF COMPLEX BEHAVIOUR

In 1972, in the first edition of her book *Reading: The patterning of complex behaviour*, Marie Clay was already showing teachers how to analyse the attempts at *reading* and *writing* of young children on entry to school and how to plan their instruction from this. She shows what we can learn from the contrasts between the 'errors' of children making good progress and those who are not. Over the ensuing years she, with her background as a teacher and psychologist, has developed and extended these ideas, always with a clear link with their implications for practice. Her work in New Zealand, and more recently in a number of other countries, has greatly influenced the programme of assessment for Key Stage 1 in England and Wales, with regard to both children's developing concepts of print and the use of running records using 'real' books to assess their early reading progress. Her Reading Recovery Programme, based on her research, has become an officially recognised way of identifying and helping children who are falling behind in reading in the very earliest stage of their schooling.

The ideas in her first book are developed and extended in the new edition *Becoming Literate: The construction of inner control* (Clay 1991). She expresses concern that there has been too little discussion of how children actively contribute to their own literacy learning. She finds 'the big debates' divisive since she claims that successful readers and writers do emerge from many different types of programme. What she regards as the crucial issue is how best we can help readers to become independent, and how we make good readers better as a result of their reading.

She stresses just how critical for learning to read are the first two years of instruction, as the formative stage for 'efficient or inefficient processing strategies'.

YOUNG FLUENT READERS

In 1969 I began a study of thirty-two young children who had entered school at five years of age already reading with fluency, enjoyment and understanding, reported in a book entitled *Young Fluent Readers: What can they teach us?* (Clark 1976). I had just completed a large-scale community study of children with reading difficulties in which 1,544 children had been assessed at seven years of age on a range of tests, and those with reading difficulties had then been studied for a further two years (Clark 1970). That study provided important information on the incidence of various features in the community and in children with difficulties. No matter how large the sample, what is not permissible from a research which commences when the children have already had reading instruction in school, and some are already failing, is to assume that any of the weaknesses that the children then show are a *cause* of their reading difficulties: they might be a *consequence* of the reading failure. I had two aims in undertaking the further research with a focus on young children as they entered school, and who were already reading. One was to consider the implications for education of the strengths of these children and their homes which had contributed to their early development of literacy. My second aim was to identify weaknesses which, in others, might have been used to explain failure, yet in spite of which these children had been successful, and at such an early age, in most instances with no formal instruction.

The findings from that study, regarding the children's own qualities and the contribution of their homes, challenged a number of assumptions at the time. In the 1960s and early 1970s it was believed that children should be sent to school ready to learn to read; beyond that was regarded as inappropriate interference by parents (or pre-school teachers) with the work of the primary school. Many teachers believed I was unlikely to find such children, certainly in *their* school! Parents whose children were already reading with understanding on entry to school were made to feel guilty not only by neighbours, but also by some teachers. Few of these children had experienced direct instruction in reading; for them oral reading had not necessarily been a step prior to silent reading; not least some had come from homes from which such children were not expected. Clearly this should not be taken to mean that other children will learn to read without instruction, but only that it is possible for some children. Nor does it mean that oral reading is not essential in the classroom for some children, but it does raise the question of for how long and for what purposes.

Of interest in this study was not only the strengths of these young children, which were in processing language rather than visual and motor skills, but also weaknesses in spite of which they had managed to learn to read and write so effectively and so early. At that time greater emphasis was placed by teachers on the visual and motor skills needed to learn to read and spell and less emphasis on the processing of oral and written language. In view of the recent attention to what is referred to as 'phonological awareness', it should be noted that these children had a very high level of ability to discriminate between like-sounding words, whether the differences were at the beginning, the middle or the ends of words (see page 92). The research also provided insights into important contributions of homes at the pre-school stage and beyond to children's developing literacy, contributions which even now are not appreciated by all schools. The most important contribution of the homes of these young children was the supportive dialogue with a caring adult, directed to many aspects of their environment, including the print around them. An extensive supply of books was not available in all these homes.

In *Understanding Research in Early Education* (Clark 1989), I have compared these young fluent readers with the group of children with severe and prolonged difficulties in reading, and set both studies in their historical context.

CHILDREN'S MINDS

In 1978 in *Children's Minds*, Margaret Donaldson discussed the findings of her researches into the development of understanding in young children. Although that book is not specifically concerned with reading, it challenges so many of the then current assumptions about young children's ability to solve problems that it has an important place in any discussion on reading. In the 1970s the findings of Piagetian research featured in the curriculum of most teachers training to work with young children. Not only were developmental stages laid out for children's thinking, but as presented to many teachers in training, these appeared to set upper limits to children's understanding at each age level. At certain stages children were expected to be unable to solve problems of number, space and capacity or to cope with abstract thinking. What is important for our present purposes is Margaret Donaldson's claim that the new evidence she presents has compelled her to reject some features of Piaget's theory. She shows that the ability to solve a problem, even of young children, is greatly increased if the problem is set in such a way as to make 'human sense' to them. However, she points out that frequent experiences of concrete activities do not of themselves result in children becoming able to handle more abstract concepts. She claims that 'the normal child comes to school with well-established skills as a thinker' (page 88) and that 'the principal symbolic system to which the pre-school child has access is oral language' (page 89). However,

> ...in the early stages, before the child has developed a full awareness of language, language is embedded for him in the flow of events which accompany it. So long as this is the case, the child does not interpret words in isolation – he interprets situations. He is more concerned to make sense of what people do when they talk and act than to decide what words mean. (page 88)

She claims that a child's first encounters with books and stories provide favourable opportunities for *becoming aware of* language in its own right' (page 91). Most parents talk *with* words to their children (in contexts within which the meaning is carried by other things in addition to the words spoken); there are parents who talk *about* words to their children, playing word games with them for example. From this some children have a head start when they come to learn to read; other children have conceptual problems to which the teacher must be sensitive. She feels that an important component in preparing children for reading is making them aware of spoken language, 'helping them to notice what they are doing' (page 97). Margaret Donaldson regards literacy as important for the child's development of understanding. However, the way it is taught is of great importance if the process of becoming literate is 'greatly to enhance the child's reflective awareness' (page 99).

In a more recent publication Margaret Donaldson considers language skills and reading from a developmental perspective (Donaldson and Reid 1985). There she argues that 'learning to read is learning to comprehend language expressed through a new medium' (page 16). She does not accept, however, either that we can learn to read as we learned oral language or that the language of books is the same as oral language with only the medium changed. The young child has so many non-linguistic cues which help with understanding in oral language, whether gesture, facial expression, or tone of voice. Furthermore, conversation with young children is usually set in a context which helps the child to derive meaning without a full understanding of the words. Tackling print requires new ways of thinking and interpretation. The 'disembedded' nature of print in contrast to speech, she argues, is one of the major problems for the young learner. In planning our teaching we must consider that even very young children:

✦ are actively trying to make sense of the world around them;

✦ come to school already knowing a great deal about oral language (though perhaps not able to speak about it);

✦ are hypothesis-testers and rule-users;

✦ have a strong desire to understand what people mean.

However, she emphasises that we must appreciate that 'the ways in which language becomes meaningful are more subtle and complex than we once supposed' (Donaldson and Reid 1985, page 19). Thus, children's earliest encounters with print should include experiences of 'public' print which is set in context and therefore whose meanings can be deduced. It is the least 'disembedded' of print; making sense as it does because of its setting, it can be a bridge between speech and 'print on the page'. In the same publication we are reminded of the evidence of Jessie Reid as early as the mid-1960s that many children come to school knowing very little of the nature and purpose of written language, and that they may therefore be confused rather than aided by some of the language of instruction used by the teacher.

THE MEANING MAKERS

Gordon Wells, in his book *The Meaning Makers: Children learning language and using language to learn* (1986), traces the implications for language learning, and in particular literacy learning, of the longitudinal studies undertaken in Bristol by his team from 1972 to 1984. At that time there was little information based on studies which looked at the same children at home, then at school. For that reason the team followed through primary school a group of children whose language in the home had been recorded from the age of fifteen months. It was hoped to determine if there are 'preschool experiences that prepare some children more effectively than others to take the learning of writing in their stride' and 'what sort of experiences at school can best help children to make up for what they have missed at home?' (Wells 1986, page xii). Gordon Wells stresses the important connection between the children's knowledge of literacy when they entered school at five years of age and all later assessments of school achievement. An important association was found between listening to stories in the pre-school years and the children's later literacy development. First, they were already beginning to gain experience of sustained written language, of rhythms and structures. Second, through stories the children were able to extend their experience well beyond their immediate surroundings. Stories were also found to provide an excellent starting point for rich collaborative talk between children and their parents (see Wells 1986, Chapter 7).

From an analysis of the language in the homes Gordon Wells suggests that there are some children who, when they start school, are not yet ready to benefit from stories read to the whole class. They have not yet learned to attend appropriately to written language under such impersonal conditions. Such children initially need experience of one-to-one interaction with an adult centred on the story. Ways must be found to make all children's first experiences of reading and writing purposeful and enjoyable, so that they are drawn into using 'meaning-making' strategies in the task of making sense of written language. While in the pre-school years talking and learning do go hand in hand, as he is able to demonstrate, such learning is spontaneous and unplanned. The richest dialogue at that stage arises out of activities in which one or both participants are engaged. It is given meaning by that context. One of the challenges for schools is to retain the strengths of such interactions while broadening the children's experiences and helping them to develop sustained and deliberate attention to a topic to make systematic learning possible.

Gordon Wells expresses views very much in tune with those of Frank Smith, Marie Clay and Margaret Donaldson when he stresses that children need to become reflectively aware of what they already know and still need to know about language. In this way they are enabled to take more and more responsibility for their own learning. From the evidence of his longitudinal study, he claims that stories have a role in education which goes far beyond their contribution to literacy learning. 'Constructing stories in the mind', or 'storying' is an important way of meaning-making for even very young children, he argues. His two main claims on the basis of his evidence are that 'children are active meaning makers and that the best way in which adults can help them to learn is by giving them evidence, guidance and encouragement' (Wells 1986, page 215).

BEGINNING TO READ: THINKING AND LEARNING ABOUT PRINT

In 1990 a very different book appeared, *Beginning to Read: Thinking and learning about print* by Marilyn Adams, the contents of which were no less controversial in their implications than some of those cited so far. As she herself states at the beginning of the book, it is about 'reading words', and is an attempt to understand fully the ability to read words, effortlessly, quickly and accurately, which she argues is crucial for skilful reading with comprehension. The book, which contains an analysis of the findings of experimental research and its relevance to practice in the classroom, is not a plea for an exclusive dependence on phonics in the early stages, but rather an exposition of the place of phonics in early reading instruction. While she argues on the basis of research evidence for an important role for phonics, she emphasises that 'the degree to which children internalize and use their phonic instruction depends on the degree to which they have found it useful for recognizing the words in their earliest texts'. Thus, of importance is 'immersion — right from the start — in meaningful, connected text' (Adams 1990a, page 10). She supports the use of writing as a way of assisting the development of reading skills and the practice from the beginning of encouraging independent writing and spelling. This she argues sharpens the children's appreciation of the phonemic structure of words and their curiosity as to how words are conventionally spelled.

Adams stresses the need, if we are to read for meaning, for speedy identification of words which have not been met before. She points out that although a limited number of key words account for a high proportion of the *total* words met in everyday reading material, they only account for about 5 per cent of the *different* words in print. Each of the remaining 95 per cent of words occurs relatively infrequently; yet the coherence of the text may depend on these less frequent words (words such as that, this, when, because). She therefore concludes that:

> ...deep and thorough knowledge of letters, spelling patterns, and words, and of the phonological translations of all three, are of inescapable importance to both skillful reading and its acquisition. (Adams 1990a, page 416)[1]

PHONOLOGICAL SKILLS AND LEARNING TO READ

Another influential book which appeared in 1990 entitled *Phonological Skills and Learning to Read* (Goswami and Bryant 1990), has already led to the term 'phonological awareness' appearing in official documents on reading. This book presents evidence from research of the need for children to be able to identify the sounds in spoken words before they can profitably experience phonic instruction which requires analysis of the relationship between the letters in written words and the sounds in spoken words. One of the researches quoted is that by Lynette Bradley and Peter Bryant (reported in Bradley and Bryant 1985) which shows that children's experience of rhyme and alliteration, which often starts before they come to school, does have an influence on their progress in learning to read and spell during their first years at school. Children were tested before they entered school on their ability to detect rhyme and alliteration, then their progress in reading and spelling was studied over the next few years. Young children were also trained to classify words by their sounds. From these two types of study it was shown that there is a causal relationship between a child's rhyming ability and progress in learning to read and spell.

THE WAY AHEAD

At the time it was published, each of the books mentioned above challenged then current beliefs about literacy, led to further research and had implications for practice in the early stages of teaching children to read, write and spell. The interrelatedness of the topics can be seen from the frequent references in the more recent books to the earlier ones selected for inclusion. As may be seen from some of the quotations I have selected, these authors had much greater awareness of the complexities of the task faced by young children in learning to read and write than some of those who cite them seem to appreciate. While each stresses a particular aspect of literacy development, perhaps one they felt was being inadequately appreciated at the time they were writing, none is arguing for one best method of teaching reading for all teachers, or that there is one best method of learning for all children. In the following chapters further reference will be made to studies such as these in the context of analysing how best to provide creative environments within which children can learn to read and write with understanding and enjoyment for a variety of purposes.

NOTE

1. There is an annotated summary of Adams 1990a entitled *Beginning to Read: The new phonics in context* (Adams 1990b), prepared for teachers by three of Marilyn Adams' colleagues.

AWARENESS OF PRINT IN PRE-SCHOOL CHILDREN

FEATURES OF WRITTEN LANGUAGE

To any literate adult the relationship between oral and written language may seem obvious. What else could the letters represent except the sounds of speech? What else could the series of letters with blanks in between represent except the words we speak? However, young children, like illiterate adults, may be interpreting the writing they see in consistent but erroneous ways. They may not appreciate the functions of letters, words and punctuation. Indeed, we may add to, rather than clear up their confusion by our use of these words, our explanations of their meanings or the limited materials we use. Even very young children 'know' the word 'letter'. They hear and use it before they come to school, but with a very different meaning from that used in teaching them to read ('letter' as in written message addressed to a person as opposed to 'letter' as in an alphabetic symbol). Thus they and their teacher may be interpreting the conversation in very different ways!

The differentiation between drawing and writing as forms of representation may be obvious to a literate adult. It should be remembered that even the conventions of drawing have to be learned by young children; they then have to come to appreciate the differences in conventions between drawing and writing as forms of communication.

A study of the development of our alphabetic writing system is helpful in gaining insight into some of the early assumptions of young children as they come to grips with the conventions of written language. Their individual development may even mirror some aspects of that development. It is interesting to note, for example, that lower case letters were a later development than capital letters and that early alphabetic writing did not have spaces between words.

It is a convention in alphabetic languages that there is a relationship between the approximate length of a written word and the time it takes to say it. The relationship between sound and symbol might have been otherwise; it is so in non-alphabetic languages, and was in the early history of written representation.

People have tried to record words in some form throughout history; amazingly varied ways have been used for written communication. Some representations are closer to what we regard as drawing, with a direct association between the features of the object and the written representation. Written communication may take a variety of forms within different cultures, and has changed greatly over the years. There may be differences in the way shapes follow each other on the page in written language, from left to right, from right to left, from top to bottom, or alternating (see Balmuth 1982).[1]

The use of spaces to represent meaningful groups of sounds is a convention we adopt in some written languages. Those of us who can read tend to believe that speech also is in the form of words, with a pause representing word boundaries. We may thus not appreciate fully the problems which confront the young child in learning to read and write. There are no such gaps in the flow of speech. This may be one reason why we find it so difficult to grasp the flow of meaning in speech in a language with which we are not familiar. We may not have sufficient awareness of the probabilities of particular structures within words, endings of words and sequences of words to enable us to split the flow of sound into meaningful units. For that reason we may think the person is speaking excessively quickly.

When children come to learn to read, they have to learn to observe new features by which to discriminate letters of the alphabet and words. Previously they had come to accept that something does not change its name or become a different object with change of direction. It is the same person in whichever way he or she faces, and the same toy however little of that toy is visible. Capital letters are more distinctive than lower case letters, and most retain their identity even when reversed. In contrast, for about a third of the lower case letters, their distinctiveness comes from their position in space. Children must pay attention to this feature if they are to discriminate between these.

n,u,h,y,m,w,b,d,p,q

In learning to appreciate the 'critical features' of letters and words, children also have to grasp the significant similarities of letters as different in appearance as 'D' and 'd', and words such as DANGER, Danger, danger.

We should not be surprised that young children make mistakes, and that a number of these are reversals. Rather, we should be impressed with how quickly most do come to recognise the necessary features that make for various representations of the same letter or word, and some of the relatively minor differences that change it to a different letter ('a' to 'd' or 'n' to 'h').

Which are 'a' and which are 'd'?　a d d d

Which are 'n' and which 'h'?　n n h h

Is it 'not' or 'hot'?　hot

Not all differences are important in distinguishing one letter or word from another; some must be ignored. For example, boldness or size of print may have other significance in reading for meaning, but not in distinguishing letters from each other.

o O o

As they become proficient at processing written language, children come to interpret a letter or word correctly from its context, even where there would be confusion if it were seen in isolation. They, like skilled readers, may not be confused by the fact that 'hot' in the first sentence, and 'not' in the second sentence are identical.

The fire was hot.
You must not go out.

In short, children must learn which of the many pieces of evidence on the page they must attend to, and which differences they must ignore as irrelevant, in order to distinguish one letter from another, or one word from another. This they must do in print, and in handwriting where the representation of a particular letter or word may vary greatly. Where children continue to be confused we need to make an evaluation of both the materials we have used and the explanations we have provided to help them to appreciate what are indeed the 'critical features' in written language.

YOUNG CHILDREN'S UNDERSTANDING OF PRINT

Before they can read and write in the conventional meaning of these words, or even know the letters of the alphabet, children may be interpreting marks on paper in consistent ways, sometimes very different from that of adults. In *Literacy Before Schooling* (Ferreiro and Teberosky 1982), Ferreiro reports her studies of young children's earliest ideas about print before they can read.[2] These include a number of the following findings.

✦ Children may begin to conceive of a difference between what is called a 'drawing' and what is called 'writing'. They may use a wavy line or a series of straight and circular strokes for writing (see illustrations on page 31).

✦ The child may come to believe that several letters are needed (or letter-like forms) for a word to be 'readable', but without any clear idea of why this varies for different words or knowledge of any individual letters.

✦ When 'writing' different words, a young child might place three or four letter-like forms in a different order. Even when they do not know their letters, and cannot read, young children may believe that something is for reading provided it has several symbols (not just one) and the symbols are not all the same. Three symbols the same may be rejected as 'not for reading'.

This says, 'Thank you for my present'.

✦ Young children's pretend writing may have some 'letter-like' forms, but also some of the letters from their name interspersed in their writing.

The illustration shows an attempt at writing by four-year-old Ross. He is clearly starting to recognise and reproduce the letters of his name which feature strongly in his concepts of print.

✦ Some young children pass through a stage of believing that there is a connection between the size of an object and the length of the word representing it. You might have some justification for forming and retaining such a hypothesis if the only words you had seen written were:

ant and elephant

bee and dinosaur

hill and mountain

They may believe that if you are older (bigger) your name would be longer. If you are aged three and called Ann and your sister aged seven is Elizabeth and these are the only words you had seen written and interpreted for you, your hypothesis might at that stage be legitimate!

✦ Some children believe you can only be reading if you are speaking!

✦ Some young children believe that you need pictures before you can read something in a book.

✦ Others think that if you change the illustration, but not the caption, what you read will be different.

✦ Some children go through a stage of believing that only the nouns, or nouns and verbs are represented in writing, not all the words we say.

✦ Young children in their early attempts at writing may not put spaces between words, even when able to represent the sounds with approximate accuracy, or may mark word boundaries with a dot or dash. Paul, aged five years old, puzzled his mother by the following in a typed message done before he could read:

EFUKANOPNKAZIWILGEVUAKANOPENR

This he read to her as:

'If you can open cans, I will give you a can opener', pointing to the appropriate letters and pausing between words.

(Bissex 1980, page 11)

She told him that writers put spaces between words. This he did in his next message, making it much easier to read![3]

Some children may go a long and complicated way before discovering that the writing surrounding them is alphabetic in nature and in the process they may explore other hypotheses. However, their attempts and ideas during this early period are far from being unstructured. By the time they enter school, or even a pre-school unit, some children will have arrived at an understanding of important attributes of an alphabetic writing system; others will not.

The four examples opposite are from young children in a nursery unit asked to draw and write the story of 'The Gingerbread Man' after hearing this favourite story read to them. Already at three years of age there are differences in the quality of their drawings and their ideas about reading and

Four examples from three-year-olds in a nursery unit, drawing and writing after hearing a familiar story of 'The Gingerbread Man'.

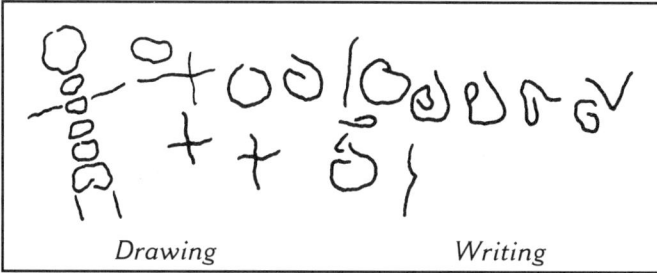

Drawing   Writing

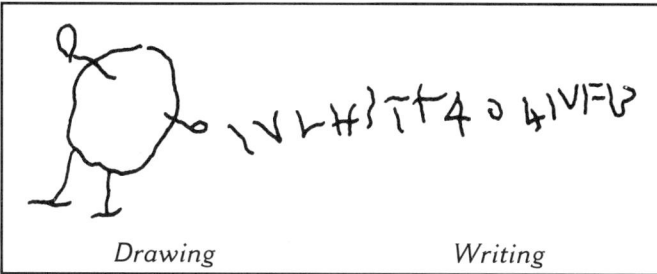

Drawing   Writing

These two children say it says, 'The Gingerbread Man'.

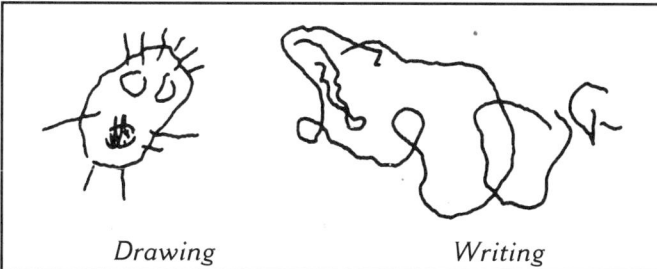

Drawing   Writing

This child said, 'I don't know how to write'.

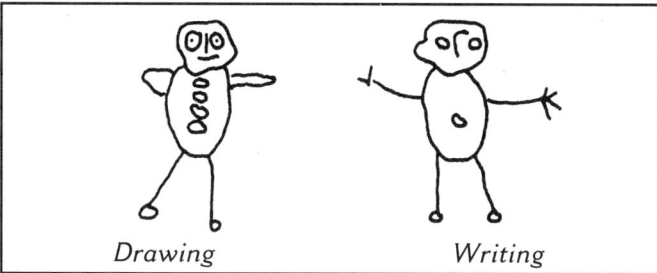

Drawing   Writing

This child asked the teacher before she started how she would know what she was writing.

writing. One of these young pre-school children who could neither read nor write was still concerned when another child drew a second picture when asked to write something. Yet another child did not want to do 'pretend' writing, because she said others would not be able to read what she wrote!

The young child who knows that a book which contains pictures cannot be read is already developing an idea of reading as a special form of response. A young child who believes he or she is 'reading' when speaking while turning the pages of a book, is beginning to gain the idea of reading, but has still a long way to go. An interesting change which can be observed in young children is a move from believing they can read or write, to saying they cannot yet read or write. What new perception of the task have they acquired for this change to take place?

UNDERSTANDING THE LANGUAGE OF READING INSTRUCTION

Some children when they come to school already have a grasp of the precise meaning of words commonly used in reading instruction (such as letters, words, sentences, sounds); others are still confused (for example between letters and numbers). Even some older backward readers retain a belief that a sentence is a line of print. I am sure you can think what sort of layout of their reading materials might have caused them to retain this belief! In contrast, some of the five-year-old children in my study who could already read with fluency and understanding on entry to school were able to give impressive explanations for words commonly used in reading instruction (Clark 1976).[4] Here are some examples of their attempts to explain words, letters, sentences:

Word
'I'm using words right now – they are made up of letters, they are things you speak.'...

'It's got a lot of letters in it and it spells something.'

Letter
'A part of a word or a postman brings it.'

'Anything in the alphabet.'

Sentence

'It's a lot of words and then a dot at the end.'

'Some words put together – if it is not a sentence it's just a jumble of words.'

The name and sound of a letter

'You mean calling S "sss".' (Clark 1976, page 52)

While some of my 'Young Fluent Readers' could give verbal explanations for the terms, others who could not were still able to demonstrate their understanding of the concepts. It is important to remember that children may well be far more insightful than their attempts at verbal explanations indicate. Verbal explanations by adults are unlikely to help young children to identify key similarities and differences in the features of print as effectively as demonstrations accompanied by active involvement by the children themselves.

THINGS TO THINK ABOUT

LETTERS AND WORDS

How do you explain to a child the critical features which distinguish a 'word' from a 'letter'? Did your explanation take account of 'I', but not 'i' as a word, and of 'A' and 'a' as both words and letters?

'Of course you know your ABC,' said the Red Queen.

'To be sure, I do,' said Alice.

'So do I,' the White Queen whispered: 'we'll often say it over together, dear. And I'll tell you a secret – I can read words of one letter! Isn't *that* grand? However, don't be discouraged. You'll come to it in time.' (Carroll 1939, page 233).[5]

LETTERS AND NUMBERS

Would your explanation of numbers take account of 'three' as well as 3? Consider just how similar is the letter S and the number 5. Possible ambiguities in written language are well illustrated in the following interchange between Paul, the young child from whom an earlier example was taken, and his mother:

> On a printed ticket that had 'No.' and a blank space on it,
> Paul wrote in the figure 1: No. 1 – 'Oh, number one,' [his
> mother] said. 'No,' Paul corrected, 'no one'. (Bissex 1980,
> page 5)

LETTERS AND PUNCTUATION MARKS

Do you make clear to young children the difference in function between letters and punctuation marks? The distinction between the purpose of letters and punctuation marks must be understood by the reader. Young children can hardly be expected to appreciate for themselves why we are expected to respond differently to marks as similar as 'l' and '!' or 'j' and '?', or to realise the importance of something as tiny as a full stop.

WORDS AND SENTENCES

Consider whether you make it clear the way that a sentence differs from a group of words, and that a sentence is not merely a line of print.

ILLUSTRATIONS AND TEXT

Do you make it clear that you do not 'read' from the pictures in a book? Children must come to appreciate the difference between the function of the writing and the illustrations in a book. Young children who watch adults reading stories to them from books which do not have pictures, or at least, not on every page, are obtaining some evidence about this relationship. Sometimes the way that picture cards and words or sentences are linked in the classroom could give young children the impression that you only write what can be illustrated.

DIFFERENCES IN DEVELOPMENT IN THE PRE-SCHOOL YEARS

Increase in young children's understanding does not necessarily move in a smooth line in the pre-school years, or indeed beyond that. The following two examples are from the same pre-school child, aged just under four years of age. They show that she was, at that particular point, making great strides in her understanding of features of print. In the first example she repeated the message to herself until she finished, sounding out as she did it. Only one month later she was sounding out initial letters of each word to be written, and painfully aware she was unable to represent letters accurately.

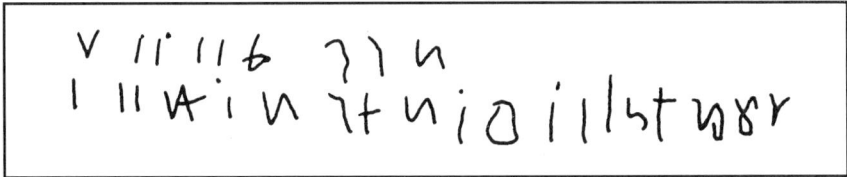

Here she said that she had written 'garage' on the first line and on the second line 'Please can I have some cars to go in it and some doors to open?'

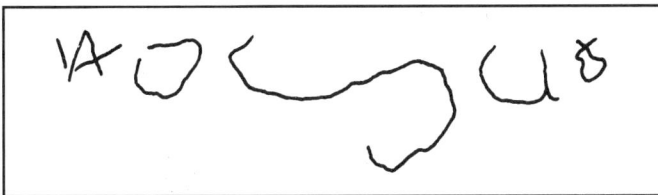

She said that she had written Christmas tree, pointing as she said it to each part of the writing on either side. She then added, 'And that's five in the middle.'

Already by around four years of age there are wide differences in young children's grasp of the features and functions of print as may be seen from the illustrations on page 36 and the children's comments about what they had drawn and written.

Children must learn the relationship between print and illustrations in books. They must appreciate the difference between letters and words, between letters and numbers and the function of the various punctuation marks which require a

Ben (3 years, 5 months)

'Writing about my brother.'

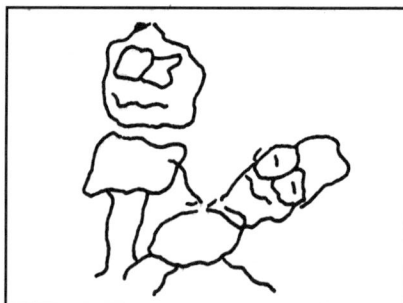

Kirsty (3 years, 4 months)

(with other similar figures)

'It says my family.'

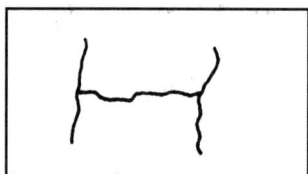

Theresa (4 years, 5 months)

'I can draw my mummy's name' (Helen).

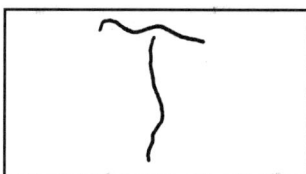

'Thats my name, Theresa.'

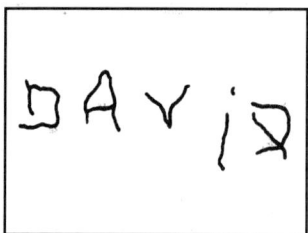

David (4 years, 4 months)

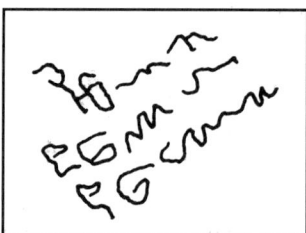

Gemma (4 years, 4 months)

'It says, for my mum.'

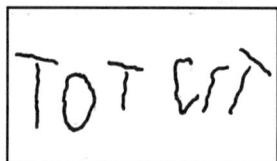

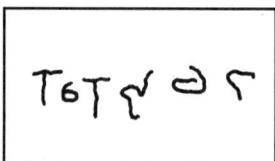

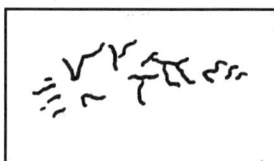

Tom (3 years, 9 months)

'It says Tom.'

'It says Sam.'

'It says Daddy and Mummy.'

very different response from the reader. Pre-school children are developing these concepts of print, to a greater or lesser degree depending on their own observations of the print in their environment, the questions they ask and the responses they get from the adults around them. Adults who observe young children closely and listen to their comments can learn so much about what each child needs at that particular stage of development.

PRINT-RELATED GAMES
IN THE PRE-SCHOOL

Insights into young children's conceptions and misconceptions about literacy can be gained from their written and oral responses to simple activities, devised to explore their concepts of print. In some reception classes most children are well on their way to appreciating many of the concepts mentioned in this chapter. Other teachers will be faced with reception classes where many children have only a very limited idea of the basis of alphabetic writing. Teachers need to plan both their instructions within the reading lessons, and the materials they choose to help the children's development and challenge any remaining misconceptions about the rules which govern alphabetic writing.

Activities such as those suggested below can be planned to engage children of very different levels of development, encouraging the children to look carefully at the print in their environment at home and school. Progressive use of the language needed for instruction in reading by the teacher, and gradually by the children themselves, during such games will lay a valuable foundation on which to build at the next stage in their early education.

GAMES WITH WORDS

Make collections of as many words of different lengths as possible, getting children to hunt for the longest and shortest words they can find. You could include their own names in the collection. Long words could be put in one box and short in another, then words with the same number of letters could be put in the same box. The more advanced children might like to count the number of letters in the words. Less advanced children could work with the shorter words, more advanced with longer words. Where necessary you or another child could write the words they find. Don't worry if the children cannot read the words at this stage. You are only trying to encourage them to be interested in the features of words. They might suggest ways you can play with the words, which could be grouped by first letter, instead of length. Some advanced children may even notice the same word written in different ways (for example, their name in capitals and lower case). They may ask you, or even tell you, what some of the words they find are.

GAMES WITH LETTERS

Collections of different forms of letters could also be made showing which are the same, and which are different letters. Letters could be sorted into capitals in one box, lower case in another, or by more advanced children into pairs of matching capitals and lower case. This can start even before the children can read, and may lead to very interesting discussions, as some children are bound to spot letters in their own names and may even know the names of these letters. Use of letter names will occur naturally in such games and should be encouraged.

LETTERS AND NUMBERS

One way of helping young children to appreciate the difference between letters and numbers is to play games of sorting out letters from numbers, with increasing numbers of cards to sort as quickly as possible, drawing attention as it does to critical differences between letters and numbers. Take care to use the correct words during the conversation about the task, including the *names* of the letters, and to listen for children who are still confused.

PUNCTUATION MARKS

Using samples of a variety of punctuation marks encourage children to find as many as they can in printed material. In this way they are being alerted to the existence of punctuation marks and can gradually come later to appreciate their varied functions.

GROUPINGS OF SYMBOLS

Make cards some with capital letters on them, some with lower case letters, and punctuation marks on others. Ask the children to sort them for you. See how they sort without guidance and explore with them the reasons for their choices, then suggest other ways of sorting. Some children may begin to observe that capital letters follow some punctuation marks. Some young children who are read to frequently at home are already beginning to observe such features of print at a very early stage, and it is possible to devise some related activities for these and for less advanced children.

NOTES

1. M. Balmuth in *The Roots of Phonics* (1982) traces the history of writing systems in general, the English writing system, spoken English and English spelling patterns. A. Kennedy in *The Psychology of Reading* (1984) gives a brief history of the development of writing systems, with interesting illustrations from different cultures and through the ages.

2. See *Awakening to Literacy* (1984) edited by H. Goelman, A. Oberg and F. Smith where there are chapters by E. Ferreiro, G Bissex and Y. Goodman with examples of pre-school children's understandings of print. In *Literacy Before Schooling* (1982) E. Ferreiro and A. Teberosky report studies of young Spanish speaking pre-school children's explorations into the nature and functions of the written language. The examples in this chapter are from children learning English, though for not all of them is English their mother tongue. I was able to collect similar examples from young pre-school Portugese children, and older

children whose development of literacy was very limited.

3. In *GNYS AT WRK* (1980) G. Bissex describes her son Paul's development from his earliest written products to his achievement of a full range of conventional spellings. Another helpful resource is *Writing Begins at Home* (1987) by M. Clay.

4. *Young Fluent Readers* (1976) by M. Clark is a study of thirty-two young children who could already read with enjoyment, fluency and understanding when they started school at five years of age.

5. Lewis Carroll's famous books for children, *Alice's Adventures in Wonderland* and *Through the Looking Glass*, first published about a hundred years ago, are wonderful source books for insights into the subtleties of the written forms of the English language and the fun to be derived from play with words. It was tempting to include more examples, but readers can discover, or rediscover them for themselves. My quotation is from *Lewis Carroll: The Complete Works* (1939).

STORIES AS A FIRST STEP

STORY READING AND LITERACY

All the following benefits from reading stories to young pre-school children have been widely recognised for many years.

✦ Telling and reading stories to young children are enjoyable shared experiences between adults and children at home and at school.

✦ Stories can widen the horizons of young children and stimulate their imagination.

✦ Children's vocabulary and concepts may be extended as they hear a wide variety of words and concepts set in meaningful contexts in their favourite stories.

✦ Books and stories, first encountered in a warm supportive relationship, may stimulate in the children an interest in them.

✦ Books read to children may motivate them towards learning to read, and sustain them through the early stages.

Most of the examples of dialogue around story reading in this chapter have been taken from case studies of two little girls aged around three years of age – Cecilia whose mother, Shirley Payton, was a student of mine and Cushla whose grandmother, Dorothy Butler, was a student of Marie Clay in New Zealand.

Cecilia was a very bright little girl with opportunity for a wide range of experiences. Cushla, in contrast, was tragically multiply handicapped. Her parents read to her from infancy, initially to try and help pacify her as she suffered endless pain and repeated hospitalisation, later because they appreciated just how much books and stories meant to her, and helped compensate for her very limited firsthand experiences.[1]

To quote Dorothy Butler:

> It seems clear that access to such a wealth of words and
> pictures, in a setting of consistent love and support, has

> contributed enormously to her cognitive development in
> general and her language in particular... Cushla's books
> have surrounded her with friends; with people and warmth
> and colour during the days when her life was lived in almost
> constant pain and frustration. (Butler 1979, page 102)

To quote three-year-old Cushla herself as she settled herself on the sofa and pretended to read, rag doll in arms and the usual pile of books at her side:

> 'Now I can read to Looby Lou, 'cause she's tired and sad,
> and she needs a cuddle and a bottle and a book.' (Butler
> 1979, page 102)

There is now an accumulation of research evidence showing that *reading and rereading stories* to young children *in stimulating settings*, where there is *dialogue between the adults and children*, has an important effect on the children's later progress in learning to read and to write. Such contexts are to be encouraged not only as enjoyable for all concerned but also as educational in their own right, as *part of the foundations of literacy*. If the stories are chosen carefully to appeal to the young children and to widen their horizons, are varied in theme and style, the children's vocabulary will be extended and their imagination stimulated.[2]

These early shared experiences of books help children to develop an awareness of a number of the features of written language, laying important foundations for the development of independent reading of complex continuous prose. As they come to have favourite authors, children are becoming sensitive to differences in style. That they are becoming conscious of the structure of stories can be seen from their retelling of favourites and their own invented stories which often include features of language and themes from stories they have heard. When at a later stage the children begin to create their own written communications, their choice of themes, the way they develop these and the vocabulary they use will be greatly enriched by early, and indeed continuing experiences of stories read to them. Thus, far from feeling guilty or wanting to rush on to the more formal teaching of reading, parents and teachers can take comfort from recent researches, showing as they do that what is enjoyable to adults and children, reading and rereading of favourite stories, is a valuable foundation for learning to read and to write – and has long-term educational value.

Story-reading sessions that develop close relationships between very young children and adults at home and in the pre-school have potential for rich dialogue. Within these settings it is possible for meanings to be extended and to observe and assess the growth of understanding of features of written language. Misunderstandings which might have gone unobserved are also shown, some of which may cause confusion to the young child struggling to understand the story. Where the setting is such as to encourage the young child to vocalise the problem, and the child is articulate enough to express the confusion, it may be possible for the adult to give an appropriate explanation. These benefits are graphically illustrated in the extracts from taped recordings of conversations quoted in the following pages.

INVOLVEMENT IN STORIES

Through the characters in books children can experience adventures and even explore and solve some of their own fears and problems at a safe distance. They can relive exciting happenings, even perhaps compensate for limitations in their immediate environment or as a consequence of some handicap which restricts their firsthand experiences. The fear and fun in the illustrations and text of 'The Three Billy Goats Gruff' (of which there are a number of versions) fascinated Cecilia and Cushla, as they did my own grandson who often talked of 'the ugly troll'. After the first reading of the story, Cushla, who was about three years of age at the time, was so excited that she picked up the book and retold the story.

> 'Troll say "Roa-oar!"'... Oo-oo, gave me terrible fright. See what happens? Troll stand on head in water. Billy goat go up hill, see 'nother billy goat... Please write troll's name

(noticing [mother] writing)... Troll fall splash plonk in water.

Troll got drowned.' (Butler 1979, page 64)

Cecilia, who just before her fourth birthday was beginning to show interest in where particular words were to be found on the page, questioned as her mother read the title of the story, 'Where, what does it say?' and was then able to point at each of the three words 'Billy – Goats – Gruff' on the title. After the story reading was completed she repeated this, then turning to the title page she pointed to the same words there.

Most cultures have a rich source of traditional stories known to the adults and loved by the children. There are now many beautifully illustrated children's books with a wide range of stories and rhymes to appeal to all ages of boys and girls (and to their relatives). Choice of books and stories may be dependent on others initially but very soon children develop their own preferences, and often ask for favourite stories to be read and reread many times. Cecilia's involvement in the story reading may be seen in her comments and her mother's responses during a reading by her mother of a familiar story, one of a series of tales about the animals on Blackberry Farm.

> **[Mother]:** (*reads*) ...he suddenly opened his eyes and saw Walter.
>
> **[Cecilia]:** (*looking at picture*) Why's he picking him in his mouth? Eh?
>
> **M:** Well listen to the story and see what it says. (Payton 1984, page 47)
>
> [*M reads on for some time*]
>
> **C:** (*looking at picture*) Why's there tees... te... um raindrops, down his cheek?
>
> **M:** Why are there tears down his cheek? He's crying.
>
> **C:** Why?
>
> **M:** Well, he's frightened. He doesn't know what this big black dog's going to do to him.
>
> **C:** What for does he not?...

[*M reads on to finish the story*]

M: ...And he waddled happily into his own dull muddy water.

C: Read it again.

(Payton 1984, pages 49–50)

Through such experiences children acquire a rich fund of ideas, a greatly extended vocabulary and an interest in and enjoyment of books. This may not only stimulate them towards reading for themselves but also support them through the initial, sometimes rather frustrating first stages of learning to read.

WORDS AND THEIR MEANINGS

Children's understanding of words far outstrips their ability to use these words with precision, as many parents have found to their cost in what they thought was a private interchange with another adult in the hearing of their young children! This may be seen in these three examples from Cecilia:

[*When helping her mother bake*]

C: Yeh... it is smooth, I disappeared it in... I disappeared it in.

[*In contrast in the same dialogue*]

M: You beat it up while I get the baking tins ready.

C: That means 'mix', doesn't it?

[*When walking home from the shops*]

C: I'm very tired, my feet are out of breath.

[*When playing in the garden*]

C: I mustn't step on top of ants must I, I hurt their feelings. (Payton 1984, page 19)

The young child who is read stories hears a rich vocabulary, with the words set in context. Words which initially may only attract by their fascinating sounds, may gradually come to be meaningful as a favourite story is read and reread. Cushla came to use effectively in other contexts expressions from the books she had heard read to her, such as 'doing nothing in particular', 'an amazing sight', 'terribly frightened', 'difficult', 'silent', 'strange' and 'ridiculous'. Other expressions such as 'bursting with pride' and 'a great responsibility' are phrases she was already anticipating within the favourite stories in which they appeared.

Many adults can recall instances when they enjoyed the sounds of long words and expressions, yet initially with only a faint, or even misleading, idea of their meaning. It is important to appreciate that young children, as well as adults, can understand, and even possibly read, words in context which they could not in isolation. Even very young children may, on hearing later readings of a story, come to grasp the meanings of more unusual words which escaped them initially. Through story-readings they may also be helped to appreciate the range of ways in which even quite common words can be used. The sensitive adult who not only allows, but encourages the child to take part, will soon appreciate any words crucial to the meaning of the story which are not understood. Initially a more familiar word might be substituted, or coupled with the long or unusual word, thus maintaining the children's interest, and at the same time extending their vocabulary.

In the first of the following two extracts Cecilia's father, while reading 'Hansel and Gretel', realises she has misunderstood the meaning of a crucial word and explains:

> **[Father]:** (reads) ...burnt to a cinder.
>
> **[Cecilia]:** A nice little doll, cinder?
>
> **F:** Cinder? Cinderella?
>
> **C:** Cinder doll.
>
> **F:** Sindy doll, no it's not a Sindy doll. A cinder is a little piece of burnt up wood or something. (Payton 1984, page 54)

In the second example, from 'Snow White and the Seven Dwarfs' it was only when playing the tape later that it was realised that the child had been studying the illustration because she had not understood the word 'wicked':

F: (*reads*) There was once a wicked queen who had a magic mirror.

C: She's nice, ain't she? (*Refers to picture of queen.*)

F: Mm, very pretty. She's got a crown on her hair, look.

(Payton 1984, page 56)

COMMUNICATING UNDERSTANDING

The child who is encouraged to retell a loved story (perhaps with the help of the illustrations) to someone who doesn't already know it (or for fun to guess at alternative endings) is being helped and encouraged to separate the theme from the detail; to appreciate the development and progression of a narrative; while at the same time to communicate enjoyably and effectively with others. The first reading of a story is enjoyable to a child partly in anticipation of what might happen and how it might all end. Subsequent readings of favourite stories are no less interesting as knowledge of what will happen and even anticipation of the actual sequence of events, even precise wording, gives the child a 'power' of knowledge. All this lays the foundation for written language as well as for spoken communication.

Young children who have enjoyed hearing a variety of stories read and reread to them, may show great creativity, even at the pre-school stage, in inventing their own oral stories. Carol Fox has recorded and analysed 200 stories invented by five young children chosen because of their great familiarity with stories read to them from books. The aim of her very detailed investigation was to find out what exactly these children had gained from these experiences. She makes the point that:

> The vocabularies of the five children are very striking not only for obviously 'literary' words ('perished', 'astonished', 'scolded', 'dismay', 'realised', 'evil', etc.), but also for the creative ways in which the children invent the language they need at any given time... Their frequent encounters with book language which is strange or unusual have given these children an experimental and creative focus on words,

and that focus is intimately bound up with the power of the
stories the words tell. (Fox 1992, page 133)

Children whose parents and/or other adults have read to
them and talked with them around books, stories and rhymes
are helped to engage in dialogue with others which is interesting
to all the participants. There is indeed evidence that discussions
between adults and young children, and between young
children themselves, in the context of books and story reading
are rich and complex. With rereadings of stories the children's
questions become more searching and their own language more
complex, showing a grasp of language well beyond that which
might be observed in other settings. In particular, the favourite
story read and reread seems to stimulate extended dialogue –
especially where the adult, father or mother (or grandparent) or
teacher is enjoying the shared experience.[3]

Adults should appreciate, however, that even children who
love stories may not always want to be read even a favourite
story. One such occasion for Cecilia was on a day when she
had grazed her finger. She was fascinated by the peeling skin
and interrupted the story reading to remark on it several times.
When her mother, after answering one of her queries about the
skin asked, 'Shall I finish reading this?' Cecilia replied: 'No, I just
want to talk to you now' (Payton 1984, page 56).

WORDS AND PICTURES

Often in books for very young children the story is carried by a
combination of words and pictures, or in some books the
pictures themselves carry a story. During discussion around the
stories the adult can alert the child to the functions of both the
illustrations and the text. Even quite young children become
perceptive, and may be critical where the illustrations do not tie
in appropriately with the story – for example where there is a
red car in the story, and in the illustration it is blue! Children
can be helped to identify the themes of the stories they hear by
discussion of illustrations which would help to 'tell the story'.
This alerts the child to the key episodes and to the order in

which they occur within particular stories. The story might even be recalled in a series of cartoon drawings highlighting the main episodes.

Sonia, like Cecilia and Cushla, had familiarity with stories from books read and reread to her from a very early age. Several factors increased the amount of time spent in this activity, apart from the shared enjoyment – her hyperactivity and need for very little sleep, severe teething troubles, then jealousy of her baby brother. When aged only 18 months she sat on her mother's knee during her brother's breastfeeding and enjoyed story reading. Sonia, who at that time became particularly attached to her father, observed him engaged in artistic and literary activities. In addition to stories from books Sonia had a wealth of stories invented for her by her father about exciting incidents in her own life, often involving favourite toys. Her first 'rabbit' stories were invented by her father; then she began to dictate incidents which he wrote down and illustrated. By the time Sonia went to school she was beginning to write some 'rabbit' stories herself to be illustrated by her father (Van Lierop 1985) – see example overleaf.

CONCEPTS OF PRINT

It is helpful as well as enjoyable when story reading for the child to sit alongside the adult, where both can share the experience of seeing as well as hearing the language of books. This encourages the children to see that the print carries the message, the direction in which it is read and even possibly to observe the words with spaces between. This is one reason why, when groups of young children are sharing a story-reading session in the classroom, the use of 'big books', commercial or home-made, may be useful. I have certainly seen them used to great effect with groups of young children in classrooms in Australia (see Holdaway 1979).

Some children, even very young pre-school children, may begin to ask about the print in books and in their environment and which signs say what. They begin to appreciate the

Extracts from a 'Rabbit' book dictated by Sonia.

he landed on a
spaceman!

4

The spaceman told
him off

5

Rabbit sat on the
spaceman'

6

Then Rabbit made friends
with the spaceman and
they went for a ride
in a moon car

7

(From New Directions in the Study of Reading, *Falmer Press, 1985 by permission.*)

different functions of the pictures and the words, even if they cannot explain this. They may begin to notice that certain words and letters appear frequently. Cecilia, when only three years of age, called excitedly to her mother, 'Oh Mummy, look at this funny book, it's got the same letter'. She was referring to the word 'the' and not to a letter; she was, however, showing her growing awareness of print (Payton 1984, page 66). When her father was reading to her she suddenly asked, 'Where, where, does it say "Heidi"?'

    F: It says 'Heidi' there... a big 'H'.

    C: There it says 'Peter'.

    F: Where?

    C: (*points to the word*) There. (Payton 1984, pages 68–69)

Children often notice letters from their own names in some of the words in the story. All these observations are to be encouraged, laying as they do the foundations of literacy. Indeed some young children may even 'catch' literacy, and learn to read in this very informal way without any explicit teaching by adults. It is disturbing that in these exceptional instances the adults should feel guilty, or be made to feel so, or discourage their children from going too far before entering school! There were many interesting insights about learning to read in my study of young children who were already reading with fluency and understanding by the time they started school at five years of age (Clark 1976). They had all, during their pre-school years, shared experiences of books and print with an interested adult. They were already by five years of age aware of many of the concepts of print, and were found to use some of the language and style of the author when asked to retell the beginning of a story they had read to interest someone else in reading it.[4]

THE LANGUAGE OF STORIES

Of particular value in helping children to appreciate features of print, and the language of books, are the repeatedly reread favourite stories. Through these the child learns one of the crucial features of print, that it says exactly the same thing on each occasion. In contrast, in a story which is told orally, while the theme remains the same the precise wording may vary from telling to telling. When a favourite story is reread, young children quickly come to recognise changes in wording made by the adult, either inadvertently, or as a time-saving device at bedtime! Some children may learn their favourite stories 'by heart' and even pretend to read them aloud, turning the pages of the book as they do, and even using a particular voice.

Children who have had a rich fund of stories read to them, even very young children, may simulate 'book language' when pretending to read; indeed, they may adopt the author's style, even when not exactly reproducing what was on the page. The following extract is from a three-year-old boy, Barrie, whose retelling of stories was recorded in his nursery school. As he 'read' he insisted on having the book, the pages of which he turned dramatically, and during which he read in a special voice, interspersed with asides using colloquial speech.

> **Retelling:** ...Now he came to a big house. An old lady answered, but, 'You can't come in Jack,' she said, 'my husband is an ogre'. And she heard 'Fe, Fo, Fi Fum, I smell the blood of an Englishman. Be he alive or be he dead I shall grind his bones to make my bread'...'

Child	Book
'They're just ordinary beans,' said Jack.	'I would be a fool to exchange my cow for your beans,' said Jack.
'They're magic beans just plant them in the garden and then they grow.'	'Ah! but these are not ordinary beans,' replied the butcher, 'they are magic beans.'
'How do you know my name?' said Jack.	Jack was amazed that she knew his name.
'Nonsense,' said the giant's wife. 'You're smelling things that's not there.'	'Nonsense,' said the ogre's wife, 'you are dreaming'... (Lomax 1979, page 109)[5]

Barrie also enjoyed information books, which were widely available in this nursery school, and from which he learned a great deal. In retelling these to a new listener he treated them as such, breaking off at various points to explain and elaborate with his own comments. Each time he retold 'The Fireman', as with stories, he used more or less the same wording, showing awareness that book language does not vary with retelling. The remarks in italics are good examples of Barrie's own speech, as distinct from book language. In one of these comments he is explaining why fire fighters put the hose up the chimney rather than down it to put out a chimney fire.

Child

Have you ever seen a fire-engine rushing through the road? One-fifty gallons of water...

Book

You have often seen a fire-engine rushing along the road... two hundred gallons of water...

Child

...and the lady says, 'What service do you want, the police, or the ambulance or the fire-engine?' 'Fire-engine.' So she calls for the fire-engine, then they slide down the pole... *So that's how they may go up the stairs*: and there's a chimney on fire... *know how they may put it up the way because if they putted it down the way they'd go on to the furniture that means that they may put it up the way.* There they are washing the fire-engine. Now they're testing all their hoses to see if they're all right. (Unpublished)[6]

The enjoyment and appreciation of book language developing in this young child was stimulated by his nursery school teacher, and the setting she provided, not as in the case of the other children quoted so far by parents. In our observations in this pre-school setting we found that some children were very successful not only in persuading adults to read to them, but also in having their choice of story or information book the one which was selected for the group!

Stories for young children frequently have repetition of

particular phrases and have a great deal of use of direct speech, as can be seen in the extracts quoted here. This helps to bring the characters alive for the children.

Nursery rhymes and stories in verse are especially enjoyable to young children. They are a valuable source of particular features of language. The children begin to hear and listen for the rhyming words and through this are becoming sensitised to similarities and differences in the sounds in words. They love to join in the reading or to fill in some of the rhyming words. As their attention to the sounds of words increases they will be encouraged to listen even more carefully if the adult makes the occasional 'deliberate mistake' in some of the rhymes, especially where the result is funny or ridiculous.

STORY READING IN SCHOOL

By the time they start school there are wide and important differences between children in their understanding of the nature of written communication, and in their attitudes to books.[7] The examples cited in this chapter illustrate the quality of the dialogue available to some pre-school children, and the understanding of the functions and features of written language which they are developing, well before they are expected to face the task of learning to read in school.

Children who enter school having had few shared experiences of stories read to them and little discussion around books, need a planned and well-focused introduction to stories in small groups. Parent helpers and classroom assistants can be valuable in providing such experiences. This planning includes not only choice of stories and illustrations, but also of which children to place within a particular group, and careful briefing of the adult who will be in charge. The children need to be encouraged to contribute to discussion about the story and to acquire the confidence to ask questions when puzzled. Only gradually will they be able to sustain the attention needed for full understanding of the complex language and development of themes in many stories even for quite young children.

It would be valuable on occasion to record the discussion around story reading to groups of children in the classroom. Such recordings can provide insights which will improve the quality of the subsequent sessions. Gradually it should be possible to introduce the children to a wider variety of stories and rhymes. Once their concentration has improved, a listening centre can give them the opportunity to hear their favourite stories many times without need for such a focus of adult attention and without disturbing others. On the listening centre they might even hear a 'secret' story which no one else knows, and which they might want to share with their friends! As their confidence grows, their attention span lengthens and their knowledge is deepened, they can become part of different and even larger groupings and yet still have their misunderstandings identified, and their contributions welcomed.

Thus, story reading should have an important place in the curriculum in the early years. Apart from its enjoyment in its own right, it can be a particularly valuable source of English for children who enter school with only a limited knowledge of the language. If they are encouraged to listen repeatedly to the same favourite stories and rhymes this will help them to become familiar with the language of books, and indeed with some features of standard English in ways which are fun, and which do not challenge them in negative ways.

CONCLUSION

The examples in this chapter have shown how rich and enjoyable an educational setting were the story-reading sessions shared by some children with the adults around them. Parents are not always made aware of just how valuable story reading and sharing of nursery rhymes are as a foundation for literacy, nor of how much they can do to help their young children in ways that are enjoyable to both participants. Some even believe that there is little they can do to help their children. As teachers, it is important that we do all we can to foster the self-esteem of parents. Over recent years there have been a number of projects linked to pre-schools and infant classes where story-books have been lent to the parents who have been encouraged to read to their young children and given guidance about ways of making such settings enjoyable to the child and the adult.[8] The father of one of my young fluent readers who had not himself been successful in school, confessed to me in some embarrassment some years after his son started school, that he had loved reading fairy stories to his children; it gave him an excuse to enjoy them himself.

Stories in the home, and in the early years in school, may motivate young children to want to learn to read and write for themselves. They may also sustain them through the early stages of frustration in their attempts towards independent reading and writing. Children who are slow readers are likely to find printed language difficult to understand, frustrating and affording little or no enjoyment. All too often, children who are late in learning to read are limited in their own reading in school to a diet of simplified texts or material below their interest level. Through stories suited to their developing interests read and reread to them, or taped for them, such children can at least continue to experience the richness of written language. In this way, their desire to acquire independent reading skills may be sustained or aroused. Continued access during their school years to stories, and other orally presented written language, may also help children who have difficulty learning to read, when they do come to write for themselves. Through such experiences their written language is more likely to be rich in ideas and vocabulary, and also to have the complexity of structure of written language, and not to be either stilted, or seem merely like colloquial speech written down.

NOTES

1. In *Cushla and her Books* (1979), Dorothy Butler paints a vivid picture of just how much books and stories meant to her multiply handicapped young grandchild from her earliest years. In the new edition of *Reading Begins at Home: Preparing children*

for reading before they go to school (D. Butler and M. Clay 1987), she notes just how much her early experiences of books and stories have meant to Cushla, now fifteen, still with her original handicaps and with even more discovered since then. Language and books are still a central part of her life. In *Developing Awareness of Print: A young child's first steps towards literacy* (1984), Shirley Payton traces her daughter Cecilia's interactions with spoken and written language during her pre-school years.

2. In *The Meaning Makers* (1986) Gordon Wells and others report a longitudinal study of the early language development of a group of children in Bristol, England, some of whom were followed through their early years in school.

3. Among others, Barbara Tizard and Martin Hughes (*Young Children Learning: Talking and thinking at home and at school* 1984) found rich and complex language in discussions around books. Joan Tough found the most complex language between young children as they retold stories to each other (*The Development of Meaning: A study of children's use of language* 1977). See also W. Teale's chapter in *Awakening to Literacy* (1984) edited by H. Goelman, A. Oberg and F. Smith on 'Reading to young children: its significance for literacy development'.

4. A detailed study of young children who could already read with fluency and enjoyment before they started school at five years of age revealed just how embarrassed some of their parents were made to feel (*Young Fluent Readers: What can they teach us?* by M. M. Clark 1976). These children were first seen and their parents interviewed when they started school, by which time they were already enjoying a wide range of books and other printed materials which they could read independently. They were then followed through their first few years in school.

5. Carol Lomax took part in extensive studies in pre-school units in a research which I directed, reported in *Studies in Preschool Education* (1979) edited by M. M. Clark and W. M. Cheyne. In one of these we made a careful study of the young

children who showed particular interest in books and stories during their time in the nursery school, going frequently to the book corner and often asking adults to read them stories. We recorded the little boy's retelling of 'Jack and the Beanstalk' (from which I have given an extract) for a television programme on learning to read.

6. This extract from Barrie's retelling from an information book is from the same recording as in Note 5. However, this example was not published.

7. In *Ways with Words* (1983), Shirley Brice Heath contrasts the attitudes to dialogue and to books and literacy of adults in two neighbouring communities in the United States and their effect on the pre-school children's interests and behaviour.

8. In the early 1970s an educational psychologist, Bill Donachy, devised an innovative programme to encourage parents in a very deprived area to play with and talk to their pre-school children in ways that would be educationally valuable. He found that the sharing of books was the best focus for these discussions. The teachers were pleasantly surprised at the effects on the children on entry to school. The parents who thought themselves incapable of helping their children were astonished at how effective and enjoyable these experiences were. These early projects took place in Scotland. Since then Bill Donachy has continued to develop such projects with parents in Londonderry in Northern Ireland where he is currently working. (His early projects are reported in *Studies in Preschool Education* edited by M. M. Clark and W. M. Cheyne 1979; the more recent work has not been published.)

The United Kingdom Reading Association has published a booklet entitled *Running Family Reading Groups* (S. Beverton, M. Hunter-Carsch, C. Obrist and A. Stuart 1993). In addition to ideas on the organisation of groups, it contains information on children's authors for different ages of children and other helpful references.

AND SO TO SCHOOL: OBSERVING AND PLANNING TO MEET INDIVIDUAL NEEDS

Some children would learn to read and write with little or no explicit instruction. However, all but a tiny minority of children should be able to acquire the foundations of literacy in their first few years in school with the support of carefully planned intervention based on the observation of their individual needs. By the time they enter the reception class young children in our print-filled world have ideas about the nature of reading and writing. Some children are already beginning to 'catch' a grasp of the relationship between spoken and written language. However, the gulf between the most advanced and least advanced children is wide even within a single reception class, and indeed any class in the infant department.

It should be borne in mind when referring to reception classes that in some schools in England and Wales children enter the reception class aged between four and five years of age; in others, as 'rising fives'; in others in the school term after their fifth birthday. In contrast, in all Regions in Scotland the age range on entry to reception class is four-and-a-half to five-and-a-half years of age. Yet so often in discussion the impression is given that there are, or should be, certain expectations of children at the beginning and end of their time in the reception class. These may take little account of widely differing age on entry, even within The United Kingdom.

INSIDE THE CLASSROOM

In order for effective observation of children's individual needs to take place, reception teachers need to evaluate the strengths and weaknesses of their classrooms as learning environments. Much information can be drawn from two research studies *Starting School: An evaluation of the experience* (Barrett 1986) and *A Good Start? Four year olds in infant schools* (Bennett and Kell 1989) each of which included observation in reception classrooms.[1]

STARTING SCHOOL

As part of the research entitled *Starting School* (Barrett 1986), young children were observed for two months, one in their pre-school unit and one in the reception class after transfer. Their parents were also involved in observing their children before entry to school and were interviewed after the children started school. The study found that teachers tended to have preconceived ideas about what a child ought to be able to do on entry to reception class, on what they saw as a 'normal' reception class child. It was felt that teachers must learn to identify the needs of individual children, both in terms of curricular experiences and what Barrett refers to as 'survival skills', how to cope in 'the big school'. This may present real problems for some children, particularly those who have not had experience in a pre-school unit, who may also be less confident in asking for help.

Over the four weeks during which they were observed in the reception class, the children came to appear more homogeneous as a group as they engaged in the same teacher-directed activities. Some children in that context came to appear *less* confident and *less* independent than they had earlier; more aware of what they did not know, and requiring an adult to confirm that they were indeed correct when they completed their work. The special interests and knowledge some of the children were found to display elsewhere, at home or in the pre-school, were scarcely evident in the classroom.

Clearly some of the problems in meeting the children's individual needs in the reception class are a consequence of the presence in the classroom of one or at best only two adults. In contrast, at home it may be possible for the children to organise their own activities and learning, yet have a supportive adult at their side. However, Barrett sounds a warning that excessive emphasis on teacher-directed activity for writing and number work, which may be meaningless for many of the children, or at the least not in response to their questions, may lead them to lose confidence in themselves as learners. She expresses a fear that the children may be 'learning' to believe that they know only what the activities and teacher expectations require of them. The achievement of some children in the classroom might be higher than they produced elsewhere; for others, what was regarded as acceptable in the classroom was of a much lower standard than these same children were shown to be capable of producing in other settings.

A GOOD START

Bennett and Kell in their book *A Good Start? Four year olds in infant schools* (Bennett and Kell 1989) make a number of claims, on the basis of their research which was carried out in many reception classrooms.

✦ There was insufficient differentiation to cater for the abilities of the full range of children; many young children were found to be engaged in what they describe as inappropriate tasks. Before their observation of a target child during a specific task, the researchers would interview the teacher to check what activities the task would involve; into which curriculum area it fitted; the teacher's expectations of what the child would gain from it, and any problems that were anticipated. After the session the teacher was interviewed to check how successful the activity was thought to have been.

✦ Teachers often failed to make clear to the children the purpose in the task they were asked to perform, or in presenting it to the child they indicated the wrong purpose. On occasion the teacher would express satisfaction with a particular task if the child actually completed it, even though the child had not learned what had been identified as its purpose in setting the task.

✦ The children's interest and involvement was said to be less when the demands were unclear, or where the teacher's expectations were low and the children knew they could get away with minimal effort.

✦ Many teachers appeared insufficiently skilled at diagnosing the needs of their pupils, and at presenting the tasks with sufficient clarity to ensure that the purpose was made clear to the children. Colouring is one example of an activity seen relatively frequently in infant classrooms, where the real purpose in setting the task may be related to reading or to mathematics; yet this may not be made clear to the child.

✦ What goes on in many classrooms could be described as 'crisis management' which Bennett and Kell feel is a consequence to some extent of an unrealistic attempt to individualise activities. They discuss both class management, and what they refer to as 'task' management. Although in many classrooms children *sit* in groups, rarely did they see the children working co-operatively in groups. Organisation and activities which enable children to learn collaboratively could release much more teacher-time for analysis of children's needs, precise explanations of the reasons for particular tasks and diagnosis of the extent to which children have understood the task and undertaken it appropriately.

CLASSROOM MANAGEMENT

From observational studies in classrooms with the focus on 'target' children, there is growing evidence concerning how their classroom may appear to many young children. The teacher may be working hard all day and struggling to give attention to all the children, whose needs are so very different from each other. This child's eye view shows that the attention may be very unevenly divided; that those who need most attention may have less; and of particular concern, that from the child's perspective, the attention from the adult, even in the teaching of reading may be very fragmentary. It is for this reason that in a book devoted to literacy learning I have chosen to draw attention to studies such as these, and to stress the importance of management skills as well as an understanding of the development of literacy, if the class teacher is to provide an environment which is at the same time stimulating and supportive to the needs of all the children.

LET'S LOOK, LISTEN AND LEARN

Clearly, some children will take much longer than others to acquire fluency in reading and competence in writing; some will have more limited understanding than their peers of what they read, even of what is read to them. Some children will be more creative in the stories they write and more effective in the information they convey in their writing. In some reception classes, even where no child can yet read with understanding, most children already have a working knowledge of concepts of print; in other reception classes that is true for only a few children. I have selected three sets of examples, all based on children around five years of age; each set is illustrative of a rather different aspect of early literacy.

CONCEPTS OF PRINT

Consider what can be learned even from these few responses of Hannah and Sharleen, both just under five years of age (see page 64). Contrast Hannah's attempts at written communication and knowledge of letters, numbers and words with Sharleen's relatively undifferentiated squiggles for words, letters and numbers. Note the significance of what Sharleen said as she produced several more squiggles for her name – 'I can *draw* my name'!

Information such as this could helpfully be dated and placed in a folder for each child, to assist with planning activities to meet the children's very different needs, and to monitor their progress over the year. It would be valuable to include a few samples of the children's attempts at writing at home and to note the context in which they were produced. These would not only provide additional insights but also a focus for discussions with their parents about the children's progress.

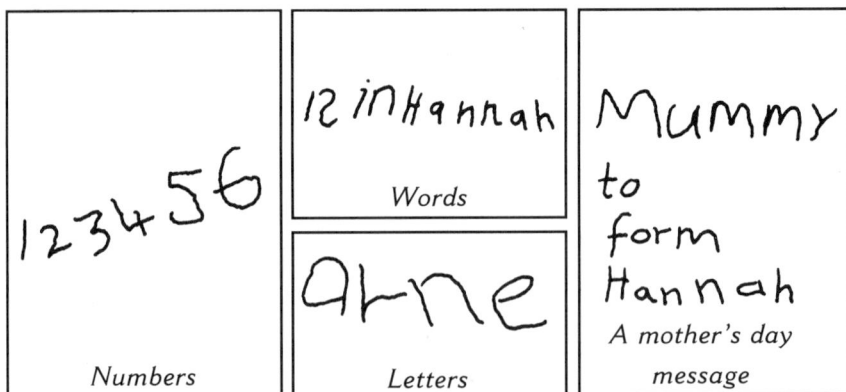

Hannah (4 years, 9 months)

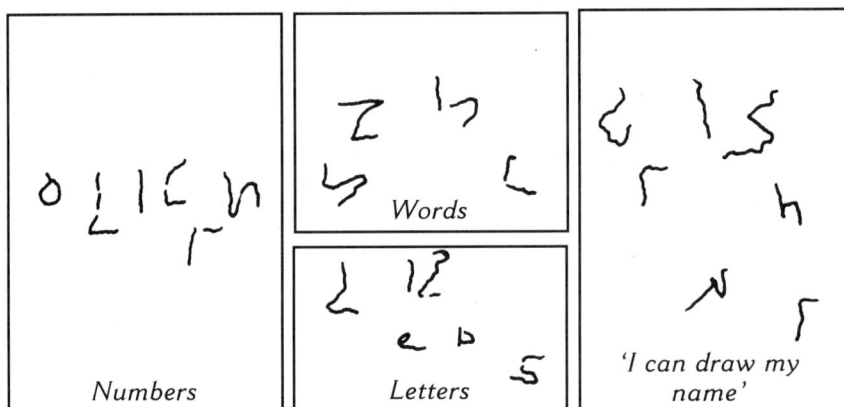

Sharleen (4 years, 9 months)

COMMUNICATION IN WRITING: THE MEDIUM AND MESSAGE

The children who produced the second set of examples are all in the same reception class. Their teacher attended a workshop on literacy I conducted recently. As a focus for our discussion I set preliminary tasks for the teachers, who were from nursery or infant classes. They were all asked to bring samples of free writing from their classes, based on a short story which they read twice to the children. This teacher, who chose as her story 'The Three Little Pigs', would be the first to admit that she had in her class a greater proportion than most reception classes of children whose ideas of writing were advanced for their age. I have selected examples of 'writing' from the following four children in her class (see pages 66–67):

✦ a boy, who could not yet write his name (admittedly a long one), and who produced only a series of letter-like forms as retelling of the story, which he believed to be writing (Example 1);

✦ another boy who, while reluctant to attempt this free writing, was delighted at what he did achieve (Example 2);

✦ a girl who could already read on entry to school (Example 3);

✦ another girl who loves writing and produces pages of writing, the meaning of which it is possible to guess (Example 4).

It should be noted that the child who produced several pages of writing was also able to recount to the teacher what she had intended to write. Consider what she already understands about the nature of written communication. Several of the others also had some idea of what they had written. In this class there were also children whose attempts were scribbles similar to those of Sharleen. All these are within a single class! Other teachers attending the workshop, with classes from nursery to Year 2, were able to compare and contrast their children's responses to a similar task. Some teachers admitted that from this simple task and the discussion around it, they had gained unexpected insights into the range of development within their class; some of the children had proved much more able in this context than anticipated. One nursery class teacher made the point that although there was a 'writing corner' in her classroom she had not appreciated previously how much she could learn from studying her children's 'pretend' writing and exploring their perceptions of writing with them.

You might find it helpful to study the examples I have included and consider how much you could learn about each of these children from their response to this one task, what questions you would want to ask each, and what further tasks would help you to gain further understanding of their needs.

**Writing by reception class children based on the story
'The Three Little Pigs'**

The three little pigs.

Three little pigs stayed in a house.

The wolf climbed on to the
chimney.

The wolf came down the chimney.

Example 1

Writing by a boy who could not yet write his name.

Example 2

Writing by a boy who was reluctant to attempt free writing. It
says, 'The three little pigs were in trouble because the big bad
wolf had a ladder'.

PRIMARY
PROFESSIONAL BOOKSHELF

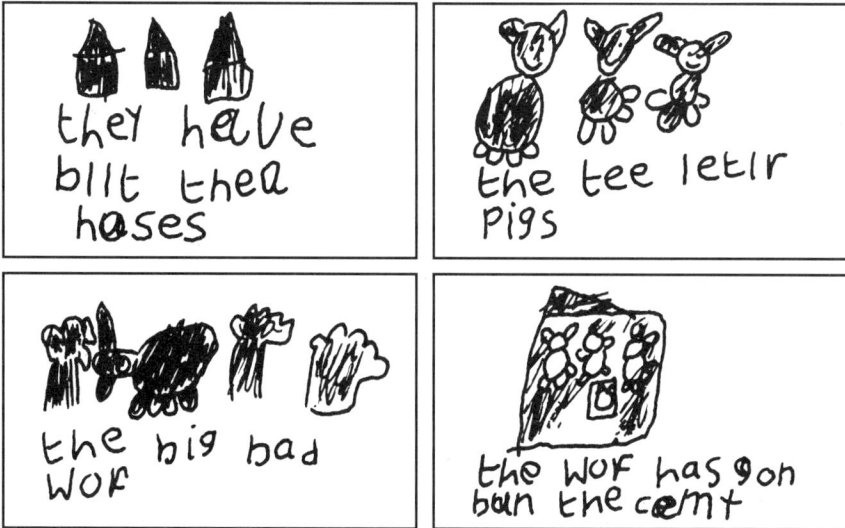

they have
bllt thea
hases

the tee letlr
Pigs

the big bad
wof

the wof has gon
ban the cemt

Example 3

Writing by a girl who could already read on entry to school.

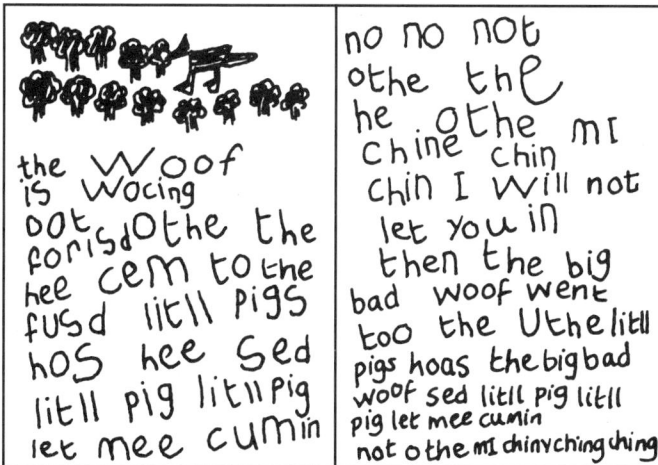

the woof
is wocing
oot
forisd othe the
hee cem to the
fusd litll pigs
hos hee sed
litll pig litll pig
let mee cumin

no no not
othe the
he othe mi
chine chin
chin I will not
let you in
then the big
bad woof went
too the uthe litll
pigs hoas the big bad
woof sed litll pig litll
pig let mee cumin
not othe mi chinychingthing

Example 4

Writing by a girl who loves writing. It says, 'The wolf is
walking out of the forest. He came to the first little pig's
house. He said, "Little pig, little pig let me come in". "No, no
not on the hair of my chinny, chin chin chin I will not let you
in". Then the big bad wolf went to the other little pig's house.
The big bad wolf said, "Little pig, little pig let me come in".
'Not on the hair of my chinny chin chin".'

UNDERSTANDING WRITTEN LANGUAGE

The following three examples have been chosen to illustrate just how advanced even some very young children can be, not only in their ability to read but also in their understanding of print and ability to articulate their understanding of what they have read. The first two examples are from boys, and illustrate, contrary to some stereotypic notions, that boys also can be very advanced in their development on entry to school. Each of these boys was in a school where many children had difficulty in learning to read, and neither came from a professional home. Both boys entered school at five years of age already able to read silently, with understanding and enjoyment. The quality of their comprehension of print is perhaps better captured in the following two extracts from conversations when the boys were five years of age than by their impressive scores on the reading tests. One boy was reported by his father to have studied a poster in a bus which stated 'FRIDAY NIGHT IS DANGER NIGHT' and commented 'It's a good job it's a Saturday!' The mother of the second boy said with some diffidence when she brought her son to school to register that he was already reading. His teacher who told me the story, rather doubting this, handed him a letter intended for his mother, to check whether he could indeed recognise any words. In the letter of welcome the teacher referred to the seven year period over which the school and the parents would have contact. The small boy looked carefully at the letter and remarked in a tone of utmost concern: 'Whew! Seven whole years!' (Clark 1989).

At the time of the interviews it did not occur to me to ask the parents for samples of their children's attempts at writing by the time they started school. I would certainly include this in any study of young children now. The children were given a spelling test, during which they were encouraged to attempt to write even words of whose spelling they were not sure. Most of the children in that study were able, before they were given any guidance in school, to spell at least some regular two- and three-letter words correctly and to make an attempt at more difficult words, as were some of the children in the samples given in this chapter. In addition, their attempts when wrong showed a sensitivity to the features of written English which make it possible to guess what words were intended, as was true also of several of the writings of 'The Three Little Pigs' shown on pages 66–67. This may not be possible in much older children if they are very bad spellers.

The third example in this section is from a five-year-old boy who had just started school. His reading of a short story, similar to those I have included in Appendix B, was recorded by one of my students as part of her practical work. He read the story with enjoyment and scarcely an error, a story he could not have seen before. To have read as he did he must have been sensitive to the complex language and range of punctuation. One error is itself interesting. Part way through the story he came to the following:

> The greengrocer's was always an interesting shop to look
> at, because of all the things written on the window
> with white paint, and all the labels.
> Some of the things were easy to read, like LEEKS.
> Some were difficult, like ASPARAGUS.
> Some were in between, like HOT PEPPERS.
> (From *Oscar Buys the Biscuits*, Ross 1985)

The word on which he became stuck was 'ASPARAGUS'. The student supplied the word, at which the child chuckled and said: 'That is difficult isn't it?'

I also have on tape, in complete contrast, that child reading from his school reading book. This particular simple scheme reader he read in an odd, sing-song voice, with little expression; I must confess it didn't have much meaning anyway!

IMPLICATIONS

It seemed important to include reference to young fluent readers in this chapter, and in doing so to stress the range of abilities possessed by some of them, since these are not always catered for, or even recognised in school. Some parents are embarrassed that their child is already reading on entry to school and are therefore diffident about informing the school; other parents may still meet with a rebuff if they do mention this. Even where teachers do realise that particular children can read on entry to school they do not always appreciate the quality of their understanding. Thus, the activities and reading material provided may not be sufficiently challenging, or a much lower standard of performance may be accepted from these children than they are capable of achieving, or may already have shown in other settings. A recent study in Denmark (as yet unpublished), has found that similar problems to those I highlighted in my study do still arise for young children who can read on entry to school, and for their parents.

A number of observational studies in the pre-school and reception class have indicated just how fragmentary, and subject to frequent interruptions are the contacts between a particular child and the teacher, including when the teacher is hearing the child read. So many teachers of young children still appear to feel they are failing if they do not hear all the children read each day. It is worth considering in what circumstances and for which children there might be better use of the precious time the teacher can devote to particular children.

I am all too aware of the pressure on teaching time, the conflicting demands on teachers in the classroom, the frequent interruptions and the very different levels of understanding of the children even within a single class. It is none the less possible to plan some activities where the initial stimulus is shared by the class, yet the tasks which follow are graded to suit the needs of individual children, or groups of children. Even where none of the children in a group could solve a task on their own, there is evidence that working co-operatively children can achieve much higher levels of understanding than any of the children could have achieved on their own. What is important for learning is that the child has focused 'quality' attention from the teacher, which even if brief is uninterrupted.

Practical suggestions are given in the following chapters, and where possible, ideas are given concerning ways in which these can be shared by the whole class, yet lead to a variety of tasks planned to be appropriate to individual children or groups of children. However, only if teachers monitor the progress of the children systematically will they be able to identify the needs of the individual children and plan in such a way as to meet these. An essential element in planning should be close observation of the children's responses to spoken and written language in a variety of stimulating situations. We as teachers can learn a great deal if *we* look and listen!

NOTE

1. *Starting School: An evaluation of the experience* (Barrett 1986) is a report of a research commissioned by one of the teachers' unions, following a survey concerning the behaviour of children starting school. For the first phase of the study teachers studied their own reception classrooms, activities and organisation, and observed target children's responses for the first month of each term during the school year. For the second phase the researchers observed target children in the pre-school unit, then as they entered the reception class. Parents were also involved in making observations of the children at home, and were interviewed. Most of the schools in this study had three intakes per year, so the children entered as 'rising fives'.

A Good Start? Four year olds in infant schools (Bennett and Kell 1989) is the report of a research conducted in three local authorities with different policies for children's admission to reception class; in one LEA once a year, in the second, termly, and in the third, twice per year. This research had two phases; for the first head teachers and reception class teachers were interviewed. The second phase involved observation of 'target' children in eleven schools. A third study, which took place shortly before the introduction of the National Curriculum, has also been a source of information for this chapter, *Young Children at School in the Inner City* (Tizard *et al.* 1988). That research involved observation of young children in inner city schools in the London area over a period of years, from the time of their entry to reception class. The researchers show how different the curriculum experienced by young children might be, between schools, between classes in the same school, and even for children of the same level of ability. They assessed the children's achievement and interviewed the parents, in addition to their own observations which give their 'child's eye' view of the classroom.

MAKING SENSE OF WRITTEN LANGUAGE

THE GREAT DEBATES

For many years 'The Great Debate' in the field of reading, and the focus for much of the research, concerned the best method of teaching reading. Controversy centred on whether 'phonics' or 'look-and-say' (a whole-word approach) was better for the initial teaching of reading (Chall 1967).[1] The advocates of the phonics approach used as their starting point the sounds of the individual letters from which simple words would be built up. The early reading books they favoured therefore, tended to contain simple regular words which the children, if stuck, should be able to work out for themselves. For the advocates of look-and-say, or the whole-word approach, the starting point was taken from the spoken language already known to the child, namely words. In the early stages the children would learn, often by repeated exposure to some of the commonest words on cards, what these words 'say'. These high frequency words, which appear in much written language, and key words for particular simple stories in the early reading books would make up the controlled vocabulary and would appear frequently within the story.

Until relatively recently most teachers used reading schemes for the initial teaching of reading, with a graded series of books, supported by word cards, often with supplementary books at each level to provide further practice with similar words in a slightly different context. The sentences in many reading schemes were relatively short and simple and the vocabulary in the early books was controlled; although the actual words chosen and the speed at which new words were introduced varied greatly from one scheme to another, making it unhelpful to transfer a child from one scheme across to another for further practice.

The schemes developed for the phonics and look-and-say approaches differ in the type of vocabulary in the early books. However, a number of schemes which initially concentrate on the learning of whole words gradually introduce phonics, to enable a widening of the vocabulary. Strict adherence to either approach, phonics or look-and-say, presents problems for the child learning English. A rigid adherence to a phonics approach means that some of the most frequently occurring words in English cannot be used in the early stages as they are not phonically regular; thus the early reading material is likely to be stilted, even lacking in meaning.

However, while the look-and-say approach may enable a wider vocabulary to be used, it leaves the child more dependent on outside help, or on guessing to tackle new words. Although words can, on occasion, be guessed from context, the short stilted sentences and the vocabulary control in the early books in some reading schemes provide few linguistic cues to help the child make meaningful guesses. Furthermore, the child who is forced to ask or guess when memory for a word fails, is not encouraged to become independent or to appreciate that there is a system behind the written representation of sounds as symbols, even in English.

Beth Goodacre (1974) found in a survey of reading schemes in use in the late 1960s that teachers tended to favour look-and-say schemes with controlled vocabulary. In the list of reading schemes in print in 1974 which she compiled there were still those she categorised as look-and-say, phonic, sentence and mixed.[2]

Some adults may recall being taught to read through the medium of 'i.t.a.' (The Initial Teaching Alphabet), which was used in the majority of schools in some areas in the 1960s, and by a number of remedial teachers. In i.t.a. additional symbols were introduced in an attempt to regularise the sound-to-symbol relationship in English for young children in the early ſhe nekst ꝑhiꞃ tꞷ dꞷ woꞅ tꞷ fiend a plæs for ſhe scꞷl, and ernest ꝏl ꝍœꞅ a littl ſhed nekst tꞷ ſhe stæbl whær emily ſhe gœt livd.

Prose written in the i.t.a. (from Reading – Which Approach? *Hodder & Stoughton, 1970 by permission).*

stages, with 44 characters representing the sounds (see example above).

Children were transferred to 't.o.' (Traditional Orthography) only when they could read fluently. It was possible to use i.t.a. as the *medium* initially yet to use either phonics or look-and-say as the *method*. It was possible in reading schemes printed in i.t.a., however, to introduce wider vocabulary. Children being taught through i.t.a. were encouraged to produce more free writing at an early age by some teachers who felt that this medium made it possible for the children to represent the words relatively accurately because of the direct sound to symbol relationship.

Several other 'cueing' systems were used in the 1960s, including 'colour coding', where every sound is represented by a particular colour, and 'diacritical marking' (see example on page 76); both with the intention of alerting the child to unexpected relationships between sounds and symbols.

These, like i.t.a., were intended only for the beginner who would later transfer to conventional print.[3] About the same time a number of controversial proposals for the regularisation of spelling for all written English were expounded. Most language specialists opposed these on the grounds that, while regularised spelling might make learning to spell easier, it would mask many clues to meaning which are embedded in their

"Traditionally one of the first tasks of the infant school was to teach children to read. It is still, quite rightly, a major preoccupation, since reading is a key to much of the learning that will come later and to the possibility of independent study. In many infant schools, reading and writing are treated as extensions of spoken language. Those children who have not had the opportunity at home to grasp the part that they play are introduced to them by the everyday events and environment of the classroom. Messages to go home, letters to sick children, labels to ensure that materials and tools are returned to their proper place; all call for reading and writing."

Diacritical marking (from the Plowden Report: **Children and their Primary Schools,** *HMSO, 1967 by permission).*

conventional spellings. Furthermore some of the proposed reformed alphabets would necessitate relearning for adults, even possibly reprinting of existing books!

There was a rapid decline in the use of i.t.a. and the other cueing systems for early reading instruction during the 1970s, partly as a consequence of the evidence from the researches of Frank Smith, Marie Clay and Margaret Donaldson (discussed in Chapter 1). Also where i.t.a. was used in school it was more difficult to maintain links between home and school in the development of literacy and to use environmental print.

However, the debates continued as to whether or not reading standards were falling; these led the government in England to set up a working party whose report, The Bullock Report (DES 1975), set reading in a much wider context, stressing the need for a 'whole school' policy towards the development of literacy for a variety of purposes.[4]

In the 1990s reading schemes are still in demand by teachers; however, those published more recently tend to have less stilted, more natural language, and a wider vocabulary, taking advantage of the realisation that children can read in context words which they could not have recognised in isolation. We continue to see equally vehement debates on whether or not standards of literacy are falling, and how children should learn to read. The controversy is now less likely to be between the proponents of a phonics approach and the supporters of a whole-word approach, or those who propose a change of medium. There are now those who challenge the need to teach children to read using conventional reading materials; who claim that for young children who can already use language, learning to read is 'natural'. In our print-filled environment some see the role of the teachers as models of reading behaviour, and providers of a supportive environment of 'real' books from which the children will learn. The adult's role would then be to respond to children's requests for information as they 'learn to read by reading, and to write by writing'. The aim in the classroom would then be to mirror the environment provided in the good home, teachers becoming more like 'good' parents in the supportive role they adopt. At the other extreme there are those who claim not only that standards are falling but also that the culprit is the 'real' books movement; that the only solution is 'back to basics'; which they equate with an emphasis on phonics.[5]

TO TEACH OR NOT TO TEACH

There is only limited evidence that standards are falling in the 1990s, and no convincing evidence that this can be laid at the door of one particular approach to the teaching of reading.[6] None the less, this rather fruitless debate of 'back to basics', equated by some with a return to phonics teaching, is still being pursued with intensity in the press and by the government.

As has been shown in the previous chapters some children do 'catch' reading, and many children enter school with a much more extensive foundation of ideas about literacy than would have been appreciated in the 1960s. That we should build on such foundations seems clear. Whether all or most children in our print-filled environment would ultimately learn to read and write without teaching is debatable. However, most children in the developed countries are required to attend school, although the age at which they start school may be anything from four to seven years of age.

Print very quickly becomes an important source of knowledge for the children in school; writing is one way in which the knowledge they have acquired is assessed. In Britain children are already 'failing' if they cannot read by seven years of age. In other countries they may only be entering school at that age; yet as adults the standard of literacy in these countries may indeed not be lower than here. A child who might fail at five might succeed at seven years of age. It is a tenable proposition that some children might be better served if, in the early stages, there was less pressure for all children, whatever their starting point, to show independent reading and writing skills, and a greater breadth to their instruction. This is not to suggest that one should merely await readiness, but rather, use all available resources for learning that are available at school and at home (including television and audio tapes), while supporting children towards literacy in the early years.

Some years ago I met an outstandingly intelligent, well-read and knowledgeable young man, who had found it impossible to learn to read when young, and who as an adult still experienced extreme difficulties in writing. Fortunately for him, he spent his early years in an educational environment which, in spite of his failure to learn to read, provided him with a wealth of educational experiences, including oral presentation of written language. Only at twelve years of age did he learn to read. With great persistence he struggled through his first book, the very large and densely printed *Lord of the Rings*! Had his education taken place in a more conventional school system one must question whether he would have retained sufficient self-esteem to persevere, or achieved as much breadth and depth of learning as he did. Although it is not possible to develop this theme further here, it does seem important to stress just how much our expectations of children are blinkered by the educational setting within which we operate and the expectations it sets for the children, and ourselves as their teachers.

In Britain, as in many other countries, we must now operate within a National Curriculum which lays down expectations for children at particular ages and stages in listening, reading and writing. This should not absolve us from the need to consider the implications of such a framework for all children in school, including those with difficulties. There is substantial evidence from classroom observation studies that many teachers are still not systematic enough in monitoring children's progress for their assessments to form the basis for their instruction. The National Curriculum can provide a start, as a framework within which to assess young children's present level of development, to monitor their progress and plan activities to support their learning.

For some children a rich diet of so called 'real' books *as presented by their teachers* in the classroom, and supported by their homes, may provide all the clues they need to enable them to read with understanding and enjoyment. If 'real' books are the main focus, then it becomes particularly important to provide a structure which ensures that gaps in the children's knowledge do not go unnoticed. For other children a supportive environment of planned activities, sensitive intervention, and a more didactic approach may be crucial if we are not to fail them.

There are teachers who feel that they can most effectively teach children to read within the framework provided by a reading scheme. It would be wrong to assume that use of a reading scheme, no matter how comprehensive it is claimed to be, absolves the teacher from the responsibility, in particular, for ensuring that the children's literacy-related experiences have sufficient breadth. Any teachers who are more comfortable with a reading scheme as the foundation for the initial teaching of reading are required to make careful choice of a scheme to suit their needs and those of the children. Some teachers allow themselves to be lured by the sales promotion for new reading schemes, and fail to scrutinise carefully the accompanying manual in which the rationale for the scheme should be laid out. All too often teachers using a reading scheme are found not to have a working knowledge of its manual. Initially at least, it would seem appropriate to follow the guidelines of the author, modifying them only later on the basis of experience.

It is important that children appreciate the system on which written English is based, the relationship between the sounds in spoken language and the symbols in written language. Instruction in phonics may help, provided it is in meaningful contexts and its purpose is understood by the child. It is not a question of either phonics, or look-and-say, or even one and then the other. Both are valuable for reading and writing in ways that children will more readily come to appreciate if the activities in the classroom engage their interest, arouse their curiosity about written language and direct their attention to its 'critical features'.

NOTES

1. J. Chall in *Learning to Read: The great debate* (1967) considers the evidence for the various methods of teaching reading. This she followed in 1979 with a paper entitled 'The Great Debate: Ten years later, with a modest proposal for reading stages' in *Theory and Practice of Early Reading* edited by L. Resnick and P. Weaver.

2. The study referred to here into the reading schemes used by teachers was conducted in 1969. The information quoted is taken from a booklet entitled *Hearing Children Read including a list of reading schemes and other materials* by E. J. Goodacre, published in 1974 by The Centre for the Teaching of Reading, the University of Reading. More recent information on reading schemes is available also from that centre, now renamed the Reading and Language Information Centre. The Centre has also recently published a folder of information on Key Stage 1

English entitled *The Child, the Teacher and the National Curriculum* (compiled by D. Bentley, S. Karavis and D. Reid).

3. In their book *Reading – which approach?* (1970) V. Southgate and G. R. Roberts compare different approaches to the teaching of reading, including phonics and look-and-say. There are also examples of 'i.t.a.', 'words in colour' and 'diacritical marking'.

4. DES *A Language for Life* (1975) laid the foundation for views developed in the more recent Kingman and Cox Reports in 1988.

5. To Frank Smith is generally attributed the most extreme advocacy of the notion that learning to read is natural and that children learn to read by reading, and to write by writing (see Chapter 1 where his views are discussed). However, M. Donaldson did not accept that there is an easy transfer from learning to speak to learning to read. Two books which provide a range of papers, one on the importance of 'real' books and the other of phonics, are, respectively: *The Reading for Real Handbook* (1992) edited by C. Harrison and M. Coles and *Teaching Literacy: Balancing perspectives* (1993) edited by R. Beard.

6. The House of Commons, Education, Science and Arts Committee undertook an investigation, the report of which is entitled *Standards of Reading in Primary Schools* (1991); vol. I is the report and vol. II the minutes and evidence. See also the paper by M. Lane 'Surveying all the factors: reading research' in *Language and Learning* (1991) vol. 6, pages 8–13.

COMMON WORDS IN CONTEXT

HIGH FREQUENCY WORDS

Why should we spend time encouraging young children to recognise the commonest words in English in a variety of meaningful contexts? There are a number of reasons.

✦ The relationship of words to spoken language is much easier for young children to grasp than the abstract concept of letters.

✦ Relatively few words account for a high proportion of the total words in written as well as spoken English. Therefore to be able to recognise and to spell these words speedily and automatically is crucial.

✦ Some of the commonest words are not phonically regular.

✦ Few of the most frequent words have meaning in isolation; most take their meaning from the words around them.

✦ They are not easily represented pictorially, as few are either nouns or verbs.

KEY WORDS FOR LITERACY

What are the commonest words in written English? In the 1960s, on evidence from research, McNally and Murray prepared a list of 'key words' common in most written English (McNally and Murray 1968). Their list of 100 key words is still used.[1]

They claim that these 100 key words account for about *half the total words in everyday reading material*. A further 100 words contribute only 10–15 per cent more of the words in everyday reading material. Beyond this there is little added advantage for each additional 100 words. It then becomes a case of diminishing returns as the type of reading material strongly influences the remaining words which will appear frequently in a particular text.

The following twelve words account for about 25 per cent of the total words:

a and he I in is

it of that the to was

The following twenty words account for about a further 10 per cent of the total words:

all as at be but are for had have him

his not on one said so they we with you

The following sixty-eight words account for another 20 per cent of the total words:

about an back been before big by call came can

come could did do down first from get go has

her here if into just like little look made make

me more much must my no new now off old

only or our other out over right see she some

their them then there this two when up want well

went were what where which who will your

McNally and Murray draw attention to the fact that even within the 200 commonest words there are few nouns. It would appear that the nouns are much more likely to be influenced by the topic. Over the years there are also likely to be some changes in the commonest nouns in spoken and written language.

As may be seen from the above:

✦ It is important to be able to recognise, and write the commonest hundred words speedily.

✦ Most of these first 100 words are three or less letters in length, so they are easily remembered.

✦ There is much less incremental benefit from emphasis on word lists beyond the first hundred.

Some additional words may be guessed from the context by an experienced reader who is following the sense of a passage, or who has a grasp of the structure of English sentences. Some words will appear repeatedly within a particular context, but infrequently elsewhere. While high frequency words account for about half the *total* words, it is essential to be able to recognise also the words which appear much less frequently and which account for over 90 per cent of the *different* words in written language. For this reason children must also be helped to develop strategies for speedy recognition of words they have not met before.

WORD COUNTS BASED ON SHORT STORIES

How relevant is the McNally and Murray list in the 1990s? In view of the gap of about thirty years since these lists were prepared, it seemed worth checking how useful they remain in current written language. Wendy Dewhirst and I asked for a frequency count to be undertaken of the words used in the 28 stories specially written for the Granada Television School series *Time for a Story* for which we were educational consultants. Each of these stories is about 400 to 500 words in length; all were written by well-known children's authors. The authors were encouraged to use language comparable to that they used in their other stories, many of which are popular with young children of primary school age. It was stressed that although the programmes were concerned with beginning reading we did not want simplified language in the stories. Two of the stories are quoted in full in Appendix B. For the teachers' booklets a check was made on the total number of words in each story, the number of different words, the most frequently appearing words and the extent to which the first 32 words in the key words list appeared in each story.

✦ At least 100 words (of 400–500) in these stories came from the first 32 in the Key Words List, in some stories many more than that.

✦ The first twelve words listed above accounted for more than the following twenty, with frequent use of most of these in the stories.

✦ In most instances the words were in lower case; they also occurred on occasion with a capital letter, at the beginning of a sentence.

✦ The use of direct speech in most of the stories for dialogue between the characters, which is very common in stories enjoyed by young children, meant that in addition there were many instances of words based on the first twelve words, such as I've, I'll, he'll, it's, that's.

These findings confirmed the value of ensuring that at a very early stage children do acquire facility in recognising these commonly occurring words at speed, whether in lower case or in capitals. Of value also would be activities which help them to recognise the relationship between the key word and related words such as:

> is – isn't, it – it's, was – wasn't, I – I'll – I've
>
> he – he'll – he's, that – that's, you – you'd

If, however, children are to understand the function of these words it is important that the activities encourage them to seek out these words in meaningful text. Since they do appear so frequently in written language of all kinds there is no shortage of material on which children can observe the first twelve words, then the following twenty words in context. It is worthwhile assessing the accuracy and speed with which all the children in your class can identify the first twelve words on the list; children who read and write these without hesitation could then be assessed on the next twenty words. I have seen children of seven years of age who still do not have sufficient confidence in recognising all these common words, or who cannot write them without hesitation. It is important not to assume that children are beyond this stage without evidence to confirm it.

PRACTICAL SUGGESTIONS

✦ Use pages from old magazines, newspapers, duplicated stories or other samples of 'genuine' written language on which children can make marks using different coloured highlight pens. Two or more children may be given the same sample of written language, and the same or different words to spot and highlight, comparing their findings. Initially some children may be better with only a relatively short sample of written language. Progressively they can be given longer extracts, and more words to identify. Each time they spot the chosen word or words, these are highlighted, different colours being used for different words so that their accuracy can be checked later. As they become more observant and confident the children will be able to undertake their own word counts without having to mark the text. Children love to show that they spotted something that someone else missed! If they count the number of times a particular word appears it becomes a challenge not to miss any, encouraging careful scanning.

✦ Show the children samples of written language with which they are already familiar, nursery rhymes or short stories for example, and encourage them to check how many of the first twelve key words they contain. You could use either 'big books' with the class or a group, or a duplicated sheet. The children are thus beginning to see these words within known contexts.

✦ Devise a variety of competitions involving the children finding as many instances of the key words in different settings as they can. This will help the children to appreciate just how common they are.

✦ Ask them to find as many different forms of the same word, such as the, The, THE, or different colours or sizes of print, to help them to appreciate the critical features of words.

As such activities stimulate the children's interest in written language they will become curious about these key words when used in direct speech, when found in stories for example in such forms as he'll, I'll, it's, wasn't, isn't. Charts on the wall of word counts will bring home just how often these key words do appear and thus make the purpose behind the activities meaningful to the children. More advanced children may be encouraged to begin analysing the context in which such words are found, the commonest words which follow and precede some of the key words. In this way they are coming to analyse the structure of the English language.

It is not difficult to plan activities for the whole class along these lines, which none the less are graded to meet the children's individual needs, and encourage them to be active in their own learning. As they become more confident the children will be able to scan for an increasing number of these words, and to find them more quickly.

Children will begin to observe these words in many other written contexts around the school, outside and in their homes.

I used this word-hunt technique recently with children aged seven years of age who could barely read – some had a limited command of English – using a duplicated version of the story *When the Moon Winked* which they had not seen before. The complete story, which I read to them before they started to look for words is to be found in Appendix B. To illustrate the quality of the language and yet the frequency with which the twelve commonest key words appear in the story I have quoted below the first eight lines of the story, circling each instance of one of the first twelve key words. As can be seen these account for 28 of the 78 words.

> Once there (was)(a) king who wanted (to) touch (the) moon.
> This (was)(the) only thing (he) could think (of)
> day (and) night, day (and) night. (He) even dreamt about (it.)
> (I) must, (I) must, (I) REALLY must touch (the) moon,'
> (he) kept muttering. (He) called his Head Carpenter (to) him.
> 'I've simply got (to) touch (that) moon,' (he) told him,
> (and) your job will be (to) build me (a) tower
> (that) will reach up (to)(the) sky.

One child became really excited and wanted also to start counting other words which he noticed were 'key' words within that story. This I encouraged him to do, choosing the words himself. I read the story to him several times, then with his new found confidence, I gave him the excitement of attempting to read it a page a day on to a tape. The few words at which he hesitated I whispered so that the flow was not interrupted. His facility had improved sufficiently, and the excitement in his voice was such, as to make his reading interesting to the listener, a new experience for him, as was hearing himself on tape!

As children gain confidence in recognising the commonest words, they should be encouraged to make up sentences using one or more of the twelve commonest words, gradually trying to include several in a single sentence. In this way originality in choice of context for the words will be encouraged. Such writing will reinforce the words for the children, and emphasise their usefulness. The key word or words chosen to be included in the sentence, should be underlined by the child and always spelled correctly! At this stage I would not be concerned if other words in the sentence are not correctly spelled, provided the child can read back what has been written. In this way the children gain confidence in using these words when thinking about something else, which is crucial for fluent writing.

ANALYSIS OF ONE SHORT STORY

In Appendix B you will find the full text of two of the twenty-eight stories referred to earlier, *One Up* by Hazel Townson on pages 159 and 160 and *When the Moon Winked*, retold by Sarah and Stephen Corrin on pages 164 and 165. I and my students have used these and similar stories extensively with a wide age range of children, and in different countries, to stimulate their reading, their sensitivity to written language and as a basis for their own writing. (Ideas for ways of developing work based on stories such as these is to be found in Chapter 10.) However, I thought an analysis of the language used in one of these stories would help clarify the points made in this chapter. I have chosen *One Up*, because I have, over the years, collected so many examples based on this story, which we used in manuscript even before it was published. You may like to analyse the other story for yourself – or even better, encourage your children to do so!

Please turn to Appendix B and read the story before studying the analysis opposite, so that you know the theme, and have a feel for the quality of the language.

ANALYSIS OF *ONE UP*

✦ Total number of words = 502

✦ Number of words accounted for by the first 32 Key Words = 147

✦ All but one of the first twelve key words is used in the story.

✦ Each of the following words from the Key Words list appears five or more times:

From the first 12 key words:

  a, and (And), he, I, of, the (The), to

From the next 20 key words:

  as, But, on, said, so (So), you (You)

N.B. Also in the text:

  he's, I'll, I'm, I've, isn't, That's

✦ The following words not in the first 32 in the Key Words list are used five or more times in this story:

  biscuits, Charlie, count, could, four, got, I've,

  my (My), only, our (Our), pyjamas, Tess, two (Two).

(Recognition of words such as these which appear frequently within a particular story can be helped by encouraging the children to scan the text prior to attempting to read the story.)

✦ There are often phrases or sentences which appear repeatedly in given stories. In this particular story the following statement appears four times, at the end of each episode:

  'But Charlie could only count up to four so he changed
  the subject.'

(When reading this story to young children, after that statement has appeared twice, if I have paused when next it was due, the children have said it for me! In many stories a phrase or sentence is repeated several times, sometimes changed slightly for effect.)

✦ However, there are 211 *different* words in the story. Many of these are used only once; yet these are important if one is to understand the story.

IMPLICATIONS

A similar pattern will be found in most written English, whether narrative or information text, with regard to the key words. Note that while the principles discussed in this chapter would apply to other languages, a direct translation of the words listed here would not provide the key words for a different language (e.g. words for the article, such as 'the' and 'a' may not be used); a word count would need to be undertaken in that language to establish the commonest words. Likewise the ordering of words in sentences varies from one language to another.

Activities such as I have suggested here are valuable for all children, and particularly helpful to children whose command of English is limited. Their attention is being drawn to the structure of written English and to particular features in ways that will help them acquire fluency in both their reading and their writing.

Emphasis on speedy recognition of high frequency words in context has an important place in the teaching of reading and writing. In any sample of written language there will be, in addition, many words which appear only once or twice yet are crucial to the meaning. Some, but not all, may be guessed from the context. To become independent readers and writers children must also develop strategies for speedy identification of words which occur less frequently, and words which they are meeting for the first time. Ways of helping them to acquire these strategies will be discussed in the following chapter.

NOTE

1. *Key Words to Literacy and the Teaching of Reading* by J. McNally and W. Murray was originally published in 1962. The information in this chapter is based on the revised edition of 1968. Ladybird now publish a Parent Teacher Guide entitled *Read with Me! Key words to reading*, by W. Murray and J. Corby which includes a Key Word Card listing 300 key words in alphabetic order with the groups of words referred to in this chapter highlighted in different colours.

PHONICS WITH A PURPOSE

A CASE FOR PHONICS

In the previous chapter the emphasis was on helping children to identify the relatively small number of 'key' words in English as whole words within a variety of natural written language. As was seen, most of the commonest words are only two or three letters in length; this may make them more easily recognised and spelled. However, as a number of the two-letter words differ only in one of their two letters, it is important to be alert for any children who are confusing words such as:

in, is, it

as, at

we, he

on, of, to, so

Were we to concentrate only on recognition of words as wholes this would leave the children dependent on others or on guessing should their memory fail them, or were they to meet such words out of context. Furthermore, children could not learn as whole words all those many words necessary for meaningful reading. Yet these also must be identified speedily if the meaning of the text is to be retained. Unfortunately, there is not a one-to-one, perfect relationship between the sounds in spoken English and the symbols in written English. This fact inevitably adds to the burden for the person learning to read and write in English as compared with some languages. The fact that English is not a phonically regular language may make the relationship more complex; it does not mean that there is no pattern in the way words are formed and the way the letters are related to each other.[1] Our aim should be to help children to develop a number of strategies which together enable them to grow towards independence in their reading and writing.

Children must learn that there is a system in the English language, not only with regard to the way words are grouped to form sentences but also with regard to the pattern of letters within words. For example, we might regard the word 'light' as an irregular word if we consider only the individual sound-letter correspondence. It is, however, consistent if we consider it in terms of what are referred to as the 'onset' (l) plus 'rime' (**ight**) features, that is **l+ight.** There are many words in English which use that 'ight' unit. One of the words in the spelling test which I gave to the five-year-olds in my study of young children who could read when they started school was 'fight'. They could already read this word without hesitation, and even at that early age some could spell it; others could make a reasonable attempt, as shown below:

fite, fitgh, fiet, fihgt, figth

Children at that stage, whatever their age, would be helped immensely – and encouraged – were they shown how useful, and regular in sequence of letters is the rime 'ight' in English. It would be worth their while hunting for other words with the same spelling pattern since there are about ninety such words (including a few exciting long ones like 'brightness' and 'nightie'). Working through analogies such as these is helpful to spelling and to reading, because in all the words with 'ight', it is pronounced in the same way. Young children should be encouraged to make use of analogies which are based on 'onset' and 'rime'; such as 'beak'/peak (a rime analogy) and 'trim/trot (an onset analogy).[2]

Through experiences of stories and word and letter games played pre-school, some young children do deduce the relationships between the sounds of spoken English and the symbols of written English for themselves. They come to acquire an understanding of the probable sequences of letters in words in the English language, as well as the patterns of words in sentences. They notice that if you build a word such as 'cat' from individual letters, it can, with the replacement of one letter be changed to 'cap', to 'cot' or to 'hat'. They appreciate an even more difficult concept, that the word 'card' can be transformed to 'car' merely by the removal of one letter or, more difficult still, that 'stand' can become sand! As they observe words they notice spelling patterns, words within longer words; they even manage to break words into syllables for ease of recognition. As their knowledge becomes more sophisticated they will even observe word families, for example words beginning with 'ba-' or ending with '-in' and so on.

Not all children will necessarily deduce these relationships for themselves through exposure to meaningful texts. They may continue to treat each word as a 'new word', or if taught phonics in isolation, they may continue to treat each individual letter as an isolated sound; both of which may be unhelpful strategies. For many children direct instruction in word analysis skills is important if they are to become independent readers. Independent reading for meaning requires speedy, accurate and effortless response to print, including words the children have not met before. Thus, the aim of any instruction in phonics should be to assist children to acquire strategies for effortless processing of unfamiliar words 'on the run' while reading for meaning, even words which they are meeting for the first time. A knowledge of the relationship between the sounds and symbols in English is a necessary but not a sufficient foundation for this. Skilful readers are helped in their reading of unfamiliar words by their awareness of the likely patterns of letters in words, their ability to see words within other words and their ability to split words into smaller pronounceable units, namely syllables. *In short, good reading and good spelling depend on sensitivity to 'patterns' of letters rather than individual letter correspondences.*

INSTRUCTION IN PHONICS

What should be the aims of any instruction in phonics?

✦ to help children to understand the spelling to sound connection in the writing system of English;

✦ to help them to recognise the common spelling patterns at a glance.

How can we help young children to make these connections, and why do some children find them so difficult to make? Two prerequisites, the importance of which are not always appreciated, will be considered here – namely the importance of hearing sounds in spoken words, of 'phonological awareness', and of knowing both the names and the sounds of all the letters of the alphabet and being able to identify them easily. Suggestions will be given concerning the kind of activities which will help children to acquire this knowledge, yet can be modified for the more advanced children in the class to ensure that they also are stimulated and challenged. It is not my intention here to set out a programme for phonics instruction.[3] My aim in selecting the examples for this chapter, and the ideas for activities, is to indicate ways in which insights from recent research can inform and be translated into classroom practice.

SOUNDS IN WORDS

To benefit from instruction in phonics children must be able to hear sounds in words; this is not as simple as it seems. When speaking and listening our attention is on comprehension (meaning). Under normal circumstances when children listen to spoken language they are attempting to make sense of what is said; thus they are not listening for individual words, and certainly not identifying the individual sounds within words. Therefore, they may have to be helped to listen for and to break the words into their constituent sounds. Many young children have not fully mastered this skill of hearing the individual sounds in words when they come to school. Indeed, some children find this very difficult, yet until they are able to do this they are unlikely to profit from instruction in phonics. Although 'phonological awareness' is a purely oral competence, children's ability to split spoken words into their constituent sounds has been shown to be an important indicator as to how well they will read and spell. There is also evidence that children who have difficulties can be helped by activities planned to encourage them to listen, and to compare and contrast the individual sounds in words.

The words we speak can be broken down into component parts, of individual syllables and phonemes. A 'phoneme' is the smallest unit of sound that can change the meaning of a word – for example, from 'cat' to 'mat', 'mat' to 'map', or 'bag' to 'big'. These words each have three letters, and three phonemes. However, the relationship between phonemes and letters is not so straightforward in all words. For example, although there are four letters in words like 'soap' or 'shop', and five letters in a word like 'light', they also have only three phonemes, because letter clusters like 'oa', 'sh' and 'igh' can correspond to a single phoneme.

There is only one phoneme difference between the words in each of the following pairs, but its position, and whether it is a consonant or a vowel, has been varied:

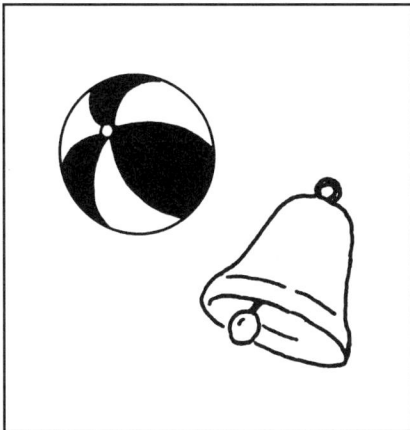

Using 40 pairs of such words and simple line drawings, we tested about 200 five-year-old children. Both words of a pair were said to the child, followed by only *one* of the words. The child was asked to point to the appropriate picture. We found that all the children could understand the task; most children had few errors; the commonest errors were in pairs differing in the ending or vowel in the middle (particularly words such as mouse, mouth; bag, back; ship, chip; cap, cup). However, these same children made many errors in a test commonly used for auditory discrimination in which they are asked to say whether the same word is said twice or two different words are said. The latter task requires more than merely auditory discrimination for sounds in words. Thus a warning should be sounded about using such a task to assess auditory discrimination in young children, or backward readers.[4]

A preliminary assessment of children's ability to distinguish sounds in words can be made as outlined above. With the help of the children, pairs of line drawings can be prepared for activities graded to help the children increase their sensitivity to sounds in words, starting with words which differ only in the initial sound. The more advanced children could help make a class collection of pairs of words which differ in this way *in sound*. Gradually pairs of words could be presented visually made up from individual letters, and the children be encouraged to transform one word to look like the other in as few moves as possible, or they could make new similar words using a limited supply of letters.

c	a	t
m	a	t

Similar approaches could help the children to see the relationship between words which include the same letter cluster or diagraph (groups of two letters representing the same sound). Instead of using individual letters for these, the two letters could initially be placed on the same card, to encourage the children to see them as a unit. Children could also be encouraged to study words within words, to listen for, and if they can, write down two words hidden in others, such as 'wag' and 'on' from 'wagon', or 'car' and 'pet' from 'carpet'.

Research findings have shown that children can be helped to increase their 'phonological awareness' by activities involving: *rhyme* – where the words end with the same sound; and *alliteration* – where words close together in speech or writing all begin with the same letter or sound.[5]

Acknowledgement of this is to be found in all the national curricula documents for English – English, Welsh, Scottish and Irish – where the value of rhyme, rhythm and repetition are stressed. There are many advantages in ensuring that nursery rhymes play an important part in children's early education. First, they are fun, enjoyable to all young children who gain confidence as they quickly become able to join in, supplying the final word of the rhyme. Second, they reinforce the feel for rhyme, and sounds within words that some children are already acquiring, and help less advanced children to listen for the similar sounds. Mistakes, in the form of alternative rhyming words could be substituted to encourage the children to listen carefully. Children could also make up their own rhymes as they become more advanced.

Word games in general, and those games which involve rhyme and alliteration in particular, give children experience of breaking up words into segments, and also grouping words together which, though different, have common elements. Listening games with supportive picture cards, and later with letter cards which can be manipulated to show the few letters that are different in similar sounding words, are particularly helpful to children with hearing or visual difficulties as they have both sources of information at the same time. Initially the focus is on words that *sound the same* and the emphasis should be on *listening for* and hearing similar and different sounds within words. English words which end in the same sound will not of course all have the same spelling. Even in the early stages in school, some of the more advanced children will start comparing the sounds of words with their written representation, and observe for themselves that there is not just one way of forming particular sounds within words; there are a number of acceptable ways. Should their curiosity be aroused, or they seem ready to explore such aspects of the spelling patterns in English, this is to be encouraged and supported. They may want to start making lists of words in which the same sound is represented by different letters – older children or adults in their family may enjoy supplying further words. From this they could be encouraged to note the commonest ways that particular sounds are represented. (As noted earlier working from analogies helps children to appreciate the common patterns within words.)

KNOWING THE ALPHABET

By the time they enter the reception class many children know a number of the letters of the alphabet; it is important to establish just how much they do know, and to build on this.

They need to be able to:

✦ recognise all the letters of the alphabet speedily in both capitals and lower case;

✦ know letters by their names and their sounds;

✦ distinguish vowels and consonants;

✦ know their ABC, that is, the order of the letters of the alphabet.

It is all too easy for some children to move through school without acquiring the necessary competence in all these aspects. Therefore it is crucial to check all these aspects with children who are making slow progress. I have seen many older backward readers and poor spellers who were still confused about at least some letters, or excessively slow in responding, to the detriment of their processing of words.

It is important to establish the names of the letters first (what they are called), as this remains constant and gives children a way to refer to the letters. When introducing the sounds of the letters it is helpful to start with consonants, as they are, in general, more consistent in the way they are sounded than the vowels, in particular the few consonants whose sound can be said in isolation, and extended without distortion, namely 'f', 'm' and 's'. In contrast, the consonants 'b', 'd', 'p', and 't' cannot be spoken without the support of adjacent sounds. Many children find vowels difficult if they are taught in isolation; it is thus easier to teach them with a consonant, for example, am, is.

PRACTICAL SUGGESTIONS

I have noted below a few activities and illustrations based on the above. They are all ones I have tried myself with children representing a very wide range of ability, including non-readers, and they require very little material.

LISTENING FOR ERRORS IN
STORIES AND RHYMES

Choose a story or rhyme with which the children are all familiar, or read one several times, asking them to listen *very* carefully as you are going to change some of the words. Initially make very obvious changes, then more subtle changes, perhaps substituting another rhyming word – for example, Goldisocks, or Jack and Jill went up the mill. The children find this great fun, perhaps because the adult is making mistakes!

MAKE AN ABC BOOK

Let each child choose a letter to illustrate. More advanced children may want to work in small groups, seeking out more unusual words and checking the spelling for themselves. When working with a class on this activity, although I give the choice of letter they illustrate to the children, I insist that the word must be spelled correctly, providing a model for the children who need it, explaining that after all we are writing a book. On one occasion, we had 'cat' and 'king' as illustrated below.

One of the children chose a knife to draw; consider how you would handle this!

AN ANIMAL ABC

Let children work in groups to make up a sentence for each letter of the alphabet, with as many words as possible starting with the same letter. They could then attempt to illustrate the sentence. This activity works well with more advanced children if the spelling of any words they want is supplied and if the occasional word which is not an alliteration is allowed. I also insist that the spelling must be correct. The resulting sentences are often original and amusing, such as the following three:

> Dd   David Duck Did Disco Dancing.
>
> Pp Peter Parrot Painted Pretty Pictures.
>
> Rr Roger Rabbit Ran Round Ryan.

I made no suggestions for the illustrations, some of which can be very imaginative (especially if you aren't good at drawing); four are shown here. How would you have illustrated these two sentences: 'Unicorn Upset Uncle Uriah' or 'William Worm Wondered Whether We Were Walking'?

Aa Angry Alligator Attacks an apple

Ff Fast Fred Found four fat fishes

Uu Unicorn upset uncle Uriah

Ww William worm wondered whether we were walking

TONGUE TWISTERS

Help the less able children to develop a tongue twister, with each word beginning with the same letter, which they must write correctly in a long line. They can then draw the face to which a tongue with the tongue twister is attached. Great fun can be had as they try to repeat it more and more quickly. Some children with whom I use this cannot make up their own tongue twisters, so we make up a few as a group, then they choose which one to write.[6]

SPELLS

Devising spells can offer another opportunity for phonic fun – and might arise from, say, a story about witches, as illustrated below.

WORDS WITHIN WORDS

Using the letters of a long word, suggest pairs of children find as many words as possible. One pair with whom I worked made seventeen words using only the letters in 'question'!

WORD SQUARES

Let children try to complete a three-by-three square with real words. This particularly appealed to one boy who showed little interest in other word games, who started making a series of such puzzles for me to solve.

t	i	n
o	■	u
p	a	t

COUNTDOWN

Play a simplified version of the television game in which contestants vie to try to make up the longest word from a selection of seven letters. Teams should be roughly matched for ability. Using consonant and vowel cards, each team in turn chooses seven cards, indicating on seeing the previous card whether the next should be a vowel or a consonant. This will help children gain a feel for word patterns as they decide whether to choose a vowel or a consonant. Both teams then try to make a word using as many of the letters as they can. Points are given to the side with the longest word within a certain time. Once the game is established more able children may be able to check that the words given are in the dictionary, but that may be too difficult and slow initially and might make the game lose its momentum.

NOTES

1. M. J. Adams, in her book *Beginning to Read: Thinking and learning about print* (1990a), provides a detailed analysis of the

research evidence relating to the place of phonics in the teaching of reading and its implications for teaching. There is also a summary of the book with a slightly different title *Beginning to Read: The new phonics in context* (1990b) from which the research evidence has been omitted.

2. U. Goswami has published the most extensive discussion of the research evidence on the role of 'phonological awareness', which now appears as a term in recent official documents. As well as *Phonological Skills and Learning to Read* (1990) written with P. Bryant, U. Goswami has written a helpful, more practical, short paper in which she addresses more specifically the role of 'phonological awareness', 'onset' and 'rime' and analogies, entitled 'The role of analogies in reading development' in *Support for Learning*, vol. 9 No. 1, 1994, pages 22–26.

3. Suffolk County Council Education Department has recently published two practical booklets for their teachers based on the research evidence discussed in this chapter. Activities are suggested and linked with the research findings and lists of publications of rhymes etc. are provided. The titles are *Rhyme: A resource for teachers of reading* (1993a) and *Sounds Interesting: Practical ideas for developing phonics in the classroom* (1993b).

4. Although I did not use the term 'phonological awareness' in *Young Fluent Readers* (1976), I devoted a chapter entitled 'Auditory discrimination and what else?' to a discussion of the problems in assessing children's ability to hear sounds in words.

5. L. Bradley and P. Bryant undertook the researches referred to here, reported in *Rhyme and Reason in Reading and Spelling* (1985). They studied children who had reading difficulties, and found they had difficulty hearing sounds in words. They also undertook a training programme involving helping children to hear sounds in words through activities involving rhyme and alliteration and found an improvement in their reading and spelling.

6. The idea for 'Tongue Twisters' was devised by Rita Ray.

REAL READING

THE READING PARTNERSHIP

By the time they start school, children's learning experiences, and literacy experiences in particular, will have been strongly influenced by their family's social and cultural traditions; these will remain a powerful factor throughout their schooling. We are inclined to assume that the purposes for which we value the acquisition of literacy are valued as highly by others, or should be. However, recent studies have shown that the expectations of the adults in some communities may be very different. In multicultural classrooms some children may be bilingual by the time they start school; others may have only a limited understanding of English. Many young children may be having to come to terms with two cultures; some, in addition, to two or more languages. An understanding of the parents' expectations for their children on the part of teachers is important if children are not to receive conflicting signals from home and school.[1] The school needs to make clear to the parents not only the general plan of literacy instruction which is being followed, and why, but also the purpose behind the various activities that their child is experiencing. All too often, teachers believe that parents of children who are having problems cannot help, or do not care. On a number of occasions when I or my students have met such parents either at home, or in other unthreatening situations, we have discovered just how concerned they are, and how helpless they feel. Teachers and parents who do manage to work in partnership are enabled to share ideas and insights with each other.[2]

By the time they enter school there will already be wide differences in the extent to which children are developing an awareness of print. Some may even be beginning to recognise a few words in context; others may be able to 'read' a favourite story with a close approximation to the original. They may enjoy sharing their favourite stories with others, bringing their favourite books to school for the teacher to read to, and perhaps discuss with, their class-mates. Links with home will be reinforced if the children are encouraged to take popular books home to be shared with their parents. They might even ask an adult to tape their favourites so that they can listen to them as often as they want, perhaps following the story in the book as they listen. Some classes may have one or more children who are already reading with understanding, who may wish to bring some of their own books to school to reread on their own, silently, and on occasion discuss with the teacher or their peers.

Some young children have already developed special interests by the time they start school on which they are keen to extend their knowledge, and even expertise which they can share with others. Their curiosity may have been stimulated by their own observations and fostered by the adults with whom they have been in contact. Young as they are, they may already be turning to books and magazines for further information, or at least appreciate that these can be sources of pleasure and information. In planning a curriculum and resources to meet the needs of a particular class, it is important to create contexts for learning which capitalise on the knowledge and experience of the children and their parents. Even among a group of five-year-olds there may be children with a fund of knowledge, indeed greater knowledge than the teacher on some topics (computers, for example, or fluency in a language unfamiliar to the teacher). It is important to provide a setting which will encourage children, no matter how inarticulate they may appear initially, to reveal the knowledge they have, and to build on this for their benefit and that of their class-mates. I know of one young boy who on entering school was fascinated by geology, and was already more knowledgeable than his teacher and headteacher; sadly this was seen as a threat rather than an opportunity by the adults! We need to be aware that even young children may have a great deal to contribute, and to provide contexts that are supportive enough to enable those interests to be revealed.

The suggestions in this chapter take account of the probability that in any class there will be some children who can help others towards a greater independence in reading and writing. There will also be a fund of information on a variety of topics among the children on which to build, and which could prove the stimulus for further explorations. The children, if their curiosity is aroused, may draw in their older brothers and sisters, parents and other relatives to provide further information which can be shared, some of which will certainly be in written form. Such searches for information are likely to go well beyond the school and home, and with encouragement will involve the local library. In this way the children will come to see at a very early stage both the enjoyment and power of written language. However, careful planning and monitoring of the involvement and progress of individual children is crucial if class projects are to provide appropriate learning experiences for more than a minority of self-reliant children.

TYPES OF TEXT

No matter how slight is the children's reading ability they should not be confined to a limited diet of books; it is crucial that they experience a wide range of meaningful, interesting reading material from the earliest stages. There are many strategies which will make it possible for them to have supported reading experience, with a teacher, another adult or other children. Environmental print, non-fiction and fiction all have a part to play and can give purpose to young children's early experiences with print in school and at home.

PUBLIC OR ENVIRONMENTAL PRINT

Notices, signs, labels and advertisements are all rich sources of print in the world around. The children should be encouraged to study these as they come to and from school, at home, on television and in the supermarket. This is the least 'disembedded' of any written language, as the surroundings help to indicate meaning. As one young child asked looking at a packet of her favourite sweets, 'Where does it say Smarties?' Children can move from recognition of the label on a packet for example, to the print cut out from the packet, to identical print, and last to the same word written out of context. Identification features on cars appeal to many boys in particular and can be compared with names in car magazines. *Children thus move from context dependent identification to the recognition out of context* of individual words or groups of words, even in different styles of print.

INFORMATION BOOKS

Some young children find non-fiction of particular interest; for all children it is an important source of knowledge concerning the world around them.

Wray *et al.* (1994) report a project which involved children aged about six years of age, who were responsible for the school flower beds. These children were asked to plan the hanging baskets which the school had decided to purchase. The children's teacher helped them to make the focus of their enquiry specific enough and provided a framework for the enquiry. The project involved consulting experts, studying other baskets, and prompted by the teacher, the possibility of consulting information books. The books available for such a task are mainly adult gardening books which in layout, size of print and language make no concessions to young children. The children worked in pairs and in this way were able to support and sustain each other's interest when the going got difficult. On occasion the children, young as they were, learned very sophisticated skills. When looking up 'Busy Lizzy' they found the entry 'Busy Lizzy – see *Impatiens*'.

> Puzzled by this they approached their teacher for an explanation. Very few teachers of six year olds would plan to introduce their pupils to the use of Latin plant names and yet, occurring as it did within this meaningful context, these

> children were fascinated by their discovery.... Experience of
> research should very definitely, we suggest, be part of the
> rich interaction with books provided in our best early years
> classrooms (Wray *et al.* 1994, page 3).[3]

Children have to learn that the language and layout of non-fiction texts may be very different from that of stories and rhymes. They are never too young to gain pleasure and information from written language of this kind. Initially it might take the form of simple, illustrated instructions on how to look after a pet, how to play a game or assemble a toy, or to check the time of a favourite programme on television. With assistance from adults or peers, the children may gradually become able to consult such written information for themselves. With help they may manage to prepare instructions for others or to write shopping lists.

Although it is difficult to find attractive, well-illustrated non-fiction books containing text which is simple enough for young children, yet accurate and appropriate in the facts they set out, it is worth seeking out such books. Some young children find them the greatest challenge towards independent reading, and in their own right they are a valuable resource for information. In Chapter 3 (pages 52 and 53) examples were given of the enthusiastic responses of Barrie, only three years of age at the time, to both a story-book and a book about the work of the fire service which he had asked to have read to him repeatedly in his nursery school. He was already showing sensitivity not only to differences between spoken and written language but also to the stylistic differences between a story and an information text. Equally important, he was gaining factual knowledge in a relaxed pleasurable way.

In many infant classrooms visits are encouraged from parents and other adults who come to talk about their work. From these discussions there is ample material from which to build 'our own' class information texts. Children can be encouraged, and helped to seek out and add further facts to books such as these. Where there are topics on which the children wish information and there are not simple enough non-fiction books in print, older children in the school might meet the challenge of devising such books for their young friends. Even in a reception class there may well be children who, with support, can prove a valuable source of information on particular topics.

The text of popular non-fiction books could be read on to tape so that they are accessible to children who have a growing interest in a particular subject, but as yet little or no independent reading skill. By listening, studying the illustrations, then following the text in the book, they may have their knowledge reinforced, and also their growth towards independent reading stimulated. The children may be fascinated by the 'big' words used in discussing their topics of interest, even to the extent of observing that some of these long words have within them some shorter words with which they are already familiar.

'Faction' is the word used for writing that deals with true events, but describes them using the techniques of fiction. In discussions with a colleague in Denmark I was shown several such books in Danish about aspects of nature, which were found to be a valuable source of information and of great interest to young children. They are also a helpful bridge between fiction and non-fiction. One of the books gave a great deal of accurate information about trees and insects, and had accurate illustrations in the form of photographs. This was brought alive for the young reader by the story format of exploration of the woods in which it was embedded.

NARRATIVE TEXT

Frequent reading and rereading of stories has an important part to play not only in encouraging children to listen, but also in stimulating their imagination and in increasing their vocabulary. It is also a helpful foundation from which they can build their own early experiences of print. Thus, oral reading to the class, and to groups within the class, should continue to have an important place in the timetable throughout the infant department. It can be reinforced by placing the popular stories and rhymes on tape so that the children can begin to follow the text as they hear the story. Rhymes, short stories with plenty of repetition and which are fun (such as the Dr Seuss books) and stories with which the children are already familiar are all valuable in the early stages. Children should be encouraged to attempt to read and reread short stories and rhymes which they have heard adults read to them. Repeated reading will give them confidence and enjoyment. They will be able to savour the language since recognition of the words will need less concentrated attention than would be necessary for an unfamiliar story. Less able children in particular could benefit from many more such experiences.

Children whose command of English is limited will inevitably find it more difficult to predict words within a sentence. Their command of the forms of written English could be greatly enhanced, in pleasurable ways, if they are encouraged to become familiar with a range of well-written stories, which contain dialogue and descriptive passages. This will also help them when they come to write.

'Big books', both commercially produced and home-made, are a valuable resource in the classroom. They make it possible to share both the enjoyment of the story and the concepts of print with the whole class, or at least groups of children, particularly those who have had limited experience with books in the pre-school years. If using such books it is useful to have a few child-size copies of the same stories, to enable the children to reinforce what they have learned in the group situation.[4]

Medwell (1994) discusses innovative ways of using computer-based story-books aimed at beginning readers. The pack she cites consists of a story-book and computer disc containing the same story. Each page of the computer story is accompanied by an oral reading of the text; this can be sampled as often as needed, and in a variety of ways. Stories such as these are an enjoyable reading resource and an introduction to information technology in early education. However, for any such innovation to provide a valuable learning experience, the initial demonstrations are crucial, both of the program and of use of the computer, followed by further discussion when some of the children have had experience with the program. Most young children will need close supervision initially, but very soon some will become experts, able to help and support others; the teacher is not necessarily the only, or even the best support after the initial phase. Parents who come into the classroom may enjoy working with groups of children at the computer. While the adult may know more than the children about the reading aspect, the children may gain confidence as they explain the intricacies of the computer to the adult.[5]

CRITERIA FOR EARLY READING BOOKS

The first books that children experience as they attempt to read will colour their views of reading and the strategies that they employ to gain meaning from written language. The following are important features of their first books:

✦ they should be appealing and eye catching;

✦ the illustrations should enhance the story, adding meaning to the words;

✦ the print should be clear and well spaced;

✦ the text should support them as they begin to read;

✦ the stories should show that reading is enjoyable and rewarding;

✦ the books should provide models of written language for their own writing.

Stories in good story books will:

✦ have a recognisable structure and be worth telling and retelling;

✦ be written in flowing rhythmical language, which is pleasant to read aloud, encouraging children to predict what will happen and become involved;

✦ have a blend of familiar and more literary grammatical structures;

✦ have dialogue which is appropriate to the characters;

✦ have a higher level of vocabulary repetition than is usual in books written for competent readers.

In short, the books should include language that children use, or hear; it should not be 'readerese'! If it is not to appear stilted there will be a variety of sentence lengths and patterns; appropriate use of pronouns and of reduced forms of speech in direct speech.[6] There is now a wealth of individual books for young children which meet these criteria, including very short, yet intriguing tales, poems and rhymes. There are many sources of information, including the Library Services.

REAL BOOKS VERSUS SCHEME READERS

The distinction between 'real' books and 'scheme' readers is very misleading. What is important is that the books have quality, something worth reading. They should encourage the children, as they are building up their sight vocabulary and their phonic skills, to use all the tools they have available, including intelligent guessing from context. If the sentence structure is familiar to the children, from their own spoken language and from books that have been read to them, they are more likely to be able to make such predictions. Some of the more recently published graded reading schemes have books which meet these criteria; there are so-called 'real' books which would not. One danger faced by the inexperienced teacher who from the earliest stages in teaching reading chooses to abandon graded readers and use a wide range of individual books written for children, is that the strengths and weaknesses of all the children may not be so easily identified. A carefully planned framework within which to record each child's progress is crucial. Those who choose a reading scheme as the basis for their initial instruction (and a great many do) thereby have a series of books graded in difficulty; their problem is to ensure that they provide sufficient breadth and variety for the children in their reading.

FEATURES OF READING SCHEMES

Features which distinguish a reading scheme from individual books for young children include some of the following:

+ they are produced with the aim of helping children to read;
+ the books are explicitly and often finely graded in order of difficulty;
+ vocabulary is controlled within and across books;
+ they may focus on consistent spelling patterns;
+ there is a single author;
+ the books feature the same set of characters;
+ there is a common format to the books;
+ there is a teachers' manual;
+ the books may be supplemented by other activities.

Not all schemes have all these features; what they do have in common is that each is intended to be a programme for the initial teaching of reading. The manual should indicate what the aims of the scheme are; how comprehensive it claims to be, the extent to which it includes phonics instruction (for example the range of vocabulary and the speed at which new words are introduced; the extent to which sentence length has been controlled).

CHOOSING A READING SCHEME

Only if you feel that the vocabulary, the language of the books, the illustrations and the themes will have meaning for your children should a particular scheme be chosen. Remember that short sentences are not necessarily simple, or even more easily read. If you do choose to use a reading scheme, having ensured that the text even in the initial books is indeed meaningful, ensure that the children are sufficiently prepared before they attempt to read the book so that they will gain some meaning from the text; do not teach on the book. Many schemes have supplementary books reinforcing the vocabulary used in the main books; some have accompanying materials which can be used for a variety of supportive games and activities.

Some teachers use more than one graded reading scheme in their classroom. This has disadvantages as the vocabulary used in the early books in two schemes may be very different, and the gradient by which new words are introduced may also be different. Book 3 in two schemes may have little in common. Thus, if you do use a graded reading scheme, to reinforce and give extended reading for children who need help, it would be preferable to use the supplementary readers for the chosen scheme, rather than introduce a different scheme. This could be supported by activities planned to help the children to approach the following book with greater confidence. In addition, their experience could be widened by supported, shared reading of individual books with a wider range of characters in the stories.

HEARING CHILDREN READ

Many teachers feel guilty if they do not hear all the children in their class reading every day. Yet, if you consider not only how time-consuming such a task is, but also how inevitably short will be the time devoted to each child, then it seems important to consider whether and when that will be the best strategy for giving children practice and assessing their progress. Provided the sessions are carefully planned, and uninterrupted, less frequent oral reading to you by many of the children might well be more efficient. Tape recording of some of the oral reading sessions could provide valuable information, revealing not only the children's responses but also the appropriateness of your interventions. Listen not only to what the child says, but to how long you take to intervene, how you respond and what you ask. Pauses long enough to give the child time to self-correct may be needed by one child, even encouragement to do so, by asking the child to look again. Supplying the correct word without fuss may be appropriate for another child, with further help at word analysis later. For yet another child, encouragement to reread the earlier part of the sentence, or to look at the initial letter of the word causing problems may be all that is needed at that stage. Teachers seem more likely to pause long enough for children who are better readers to self-correct, and to encourage them to do so; in contrast they are likely to intervene quickly with poorer readers, thus depriving them of encouragement to move towards independent reading. Children should not be encouraged to skip words they find too difficult, but to take time to study them, then reread the phrase or sentence to appreciate the word in context. Meaningful experiences with words are important to the acquisition of their spelling as well as their meaning.

When you first take 'running records' as a way of monitoring children's oral reading progress, it may help to record the session. You may then find it easier to note the strategies the child is using to make sense of the text, and what the child does when problems arise. The introduction of 'running records' as part of the Key Stage 1 assessment in the National Curriculum is a valuable innovation. From these a check can be made both on the appropriateness of the reading book for particular children and on the extent to which the strategies they employ are helping them towards becoming independent readers.[7]

If a child is making frequent errors during an oral reading session, then a change to a simpler book may be needed, or some strategy of supported reading which helps to retain the meaning of the passage. The adult could, for example, initially read parts of the sentence, pausing for the child to supply some of the words. On rereading the child could be encouraged to read progressively more of the words until confidence is regained, and meaning is retained in the text. One approach which works well with some older children with difficulties is for an adult to record on tape part of the story, with deliberate mistakes introduced. The child can then be challenged to spot the mistakes while following the text in the book. Some children with difficulties enjoy the experience of hearing the adult make mistakes! This can be graded both for the difficulty level of the story and the errors which are inserted. More advanced readers may also enjoy preparing such tapes for each other. It should be remembered that it is possible even for an adult to read a passage without errors, yet so slowly that meaning is lost. Thus errorless reading is not a sufficient goal. Any oral reading should be for a purpose, understood by you and by the child. Parents and other adults may appreciate some guidance on ways of helping and supporting children when hearing them read.

There are many ways of increasing the oral reading practice that young children have; the teacher does not always have to be the audience. Indeed, on occasion a peer may be a more sensitive or acceptable teacher to a child with difficulties. If children are encouraged to read in pairs the more competent reader may support the less able. As their reading improves children may enjoy reading to each other, particularly if they have at least some familiarity with the story. The following extract is from a recording taken in a reception classroom. The teacher of this class has read many poems to the children who know some of them very well.

> Here, Reid and Helen sit together and decide which poem they will read; this act of choosing is itself a significant part of learning to read, because it involves a commitment on the part of the reader to the text: ...Eventually they opt for 'Down Behind the Dustbin' and Reid begins to read aloud. Helen interrupts him, when he reads 'Jim' instead of 'Sid'. She knows the verse goes differently:
>
> Reid: 'Down behind the dustbin
>
>   I met a dog called Jim
>
>   He said he didn't know me –'
>
> Helen: Not Jim. Sid....
>
> Reid asks for clarification:
>
> Reid: What? I can't hear what you're saying.
>
> and Helen tells him the correct version:
>
> Helen: 'Down behind the dustbin
>
>   I met a dog called Sid
>
>   He said he didn't know me
>
>   But I said he surely did.'
>
> Reid has now heard the rhyme correctly and he has another go...
>
> (Minns 1990, pages 72–73)

CONFIDENT READERS

When children reach a certain level of proficiency, there are more fruitful ways of spending your instruction time with them than asking them to read a book which you have in front of you. Practice in reading aloud would be better gained from reading to a real audience, or reading a story on to tape to be played to other children. Such children may enjoy shared reading with a friend, or supporting a less advanced child as they read a favourite story, one which is challenging for the more able, and slightly too difficult for the less able to read unsupported.

As soon as they can comfortably do so, children should be encouraged to spend time reading silently, or initially, softly to themselves. It is then possible to check whether they have understood and, equally important, enjoyed what they have read, by discussing the content with them, and to find out whether and why they would like to read another book by the same author. Children should be encouraged to develop their own preferences for stories, and style, to seek out books by their favourite authors. They will enjoy discussing why they have particular preferences, and keeping annotated records of the books they have read. In one class with which I worked we had secret ballots to determine the class favourites – both books and authors.

It is important to ensure that children have sufficient breadth of experience of books even from the early stages. The class library in a reception class may not be extensive enough for the most advanced and widely-read children, who may need access to other sources for both fiction and non-fiction books to challenge and interest them. Children may make mistakes because they are bored, rather than because they cannot manage a book! When children are learning to read, they need experience of books which are at the correct level of difficulty so that they are a challenge; yet, with the strategies you are encouraging them to develop, success will be possible. Repeated rereadings of books they enjoy will not only help the children's appreciation of syntax, but also help their own writing.

The teacher is not the only source of help to the children, no matter how young they are. Other children in the class, and older children are a valuable aid in many ways which will provide new learning experiences for both. Tape recordings are available for a wide range of literature and can extend children's experiences, perhaps encouraging some to attempt more advanced books for themselves. Increasingly complex software is appearing on the market which provides children with the flexible opportunities for hearing, seeing and responding to print in ways and at a speed which is appropriate for their level. What is important is that such materials are carefully evaluated, and that the children's initial experiences with them are monitored to ensure they are not merely playing around with the materials but having enjoyable and valuable learning experience.

NOTES

1. Shirley Brice Heath describes in her widely acclaimed book *Ways with Words: Language, life and work in communities and classrooms* (1983) the contrasting expectations of literacy in two neighbouring communities in The United States. More recently Hilary Minns, headteacher of a school in a multicultural community in Coventry, made a detailed study of five of the four-year-old children, from very different cultural backgrounds, as they were entering her school. In *Read it to Me Now! Learning at home and at school* (1990), she compares the literacy experiences of these young children at home and in school.

2. Helpful information on working with parents, and suggestions for authors whose books appeal to young children is to be found in *Running Family Reading Groups* (1993) by Sue Beverton, Morag Hunter-Carsch, Cecilia Obrist and Ann Stuart.

3. *Language and Literacy News* from UKRA, Spring 1994 No. 13 contains two articles reporting projects undertaken by young children. In both the authors consider the structure and support

provided by the teacher. In the first article, 'Young researchers at work' pages 2–3, David Wray, Maureen Lewis and Caroline Cox discuss a research project into hanging baskets involving six-year-olds (see Note 5).

4. In *Foundations of Literacy* (1979), Don Holdaway illustrates ways in which 'Big books' and 'shared reading' can be used effectively in the classroom.

5. (See Note 3) In the second article from *Language and Literacy News*, 'Using the Sherston naughty stories', pages 4–5, Jane Medwell describes the introduction of a novel computer program into a class of beginning readers.

6. Katharine Perera in 'The "good book": linguistic aspects' from *Teaching Literacy: Balancing perspectives* (1993) edited by Roger Beard, considers criteria on which to judge books for young children learning to read. She also provides an analysis of several reading schemes and compares these with individual books. Gervase Phinn, in 'Choosing books for young readers: habituated to the vast' in *The Reading for Real Handbook* (1992) edited by Colin Harrison and Martin Coles, considers the features to look for in choosing books for young children, providing an extensive reference list for the teacher. Some of the points made in this chapter have been taken from these publications. The Reading and Language Information Centre at the University of Reading has also published a helpful guide by Cliff Moon called *Individualised Reading: A teacher guide to readability at Key Stages 1 and 2* (1993).

7. Detailed guidance on ways of assessing progress in reading and writing of young literacy learners, including the use of 'running records' is to be found in Marie Clay's book, *An Observation Survey of Early Literacy Achievement* (1993).

THE READING WRITING CONNECTION

It is important that children are encouraged to write, as well as to read, from the earliest stages in the classroom. Each activity supports the other; together they give children information about words from slightly different perspectives. To read a word involves only recognition; spelling, in contrast, requires recall of each letter within the word, and in the correct order.

THE FOUNDATIONS OF SPELLING

Children need to appreciate that writing does not represent objects as does drawing; writing, in contrast, is a visual representation of spoken language. In their early attempts at writing children may merely produce a series of scribbles, letterlike forms or groups of these. A few letters may be included, perhaps letters from their names (see Chapter 2). Then they begin to realise that at least some parts of a spoken sentence are written down. However, at this stage they may only represent the initial letter of each word, or only nouns or a few key words. They must learn to identify the speech sounds as discrete entities and to classify and group these.

As children come to learn that letters have sounds they will be able, if they listen carefully, to hear the sounds within words; these they may represent in their spelling. Children's beginning spelling may be mainly phonetic (sound by sound), rather than as whole words or morphemes (meaningful parts of words). It is often strongly influenced by pronunciation.

Learning to represent vowels presents the greatest problems, as vowel sounds are continuous with, and are greatly influenced by, the neighbouring sounds; this makes it difficult to isolate them. For this reason children's earliest attempts may represent the consonants more accurately than the vowels, for example:

WRK	STRT	BRD	TABIL	WOCT
work	start	bird	table	watched

The spelling may use the letter names for the vowels as in:

KAM	LADE	FEL	GOWT
came	lady	feel	goat

To adults, children's early 'creative' or invented spellings may look bizarre, for example:

WNS	APNA	TM
once	upon a	time

Their spellings are based on a reasonable principle; that spelling represents sounds, and that similar sounds may have similar spellings, which they will later learn is not always the case in written English. When creative spellers are faced with the contrast between their spelling and the standard form which they can read, they often see nothing wrong with either, they simply do not assume that the two must be alike. Transitional spellings that begin to show some features of conventional spelling and the probabilities of certain letters following others in written English may become apparent among the non-standard representations.[1] It should be remembered that standardised spelling is relatively recent. Until the eighteenth century the spelling of adults, like children now, was 'creative', even of their names.

Children have to come to appreciate that in the written form of a word not all the sounds are necessarily represented, and that some words don't look the way they sound. As children are helped to develop a sensitivity to the sequential probabilities within words in English (the ways that certain letters are likely to follow others), their spelling will become more easily read by others and will begin to approximate standardised spelling.

Consider the free writing by the very advanced five-year-old child of 'The Three Little Pigs' on page 67 (Example 4). Although there are a number of words incorrectly spelled, she is already on the way to becoming a good speller, and even at this early stage it is possible to guess at what she means. Contrast that with the attempt below by a twelve-year-old boy who has made little headway towards representing spoken English in written form. He does not always even manage to make the break between words in the correct place, making it difficult to guess the meaning of his writing even of a dictated passage.

> lat one nit my frend woct me saning wud you injon atril run in my heleptr. I had scersly scramdeld in to my trasut be fur we wer away The lits of the sitiy god deneeth the stars abuv. I was be cining to wunder a but uwer berten ashon wen I cotsit....
>
> (Clark *et al.* 1982, page 73)

The passage that was dictated read as follows:

> Late one night my friend woke me saying 'Would you enjoy a trial-run in my new helicopter?'
>
> I had scarcely scrambled into my track-suit before we were away. The lights of the city glowed beneath: the stars above. I was beginning to wonder about our destination when I caught sight...
>
> (Peters 1970, page 78)

Thus consider the problems such a child will have in producing a written composition when he has to think about content as well as spelling.[2]

ANALYSIS OF EARLY WRITING

In preparation for a workshop on literacy which I conducted with all the teachers in an inner city primary school I asked the teachers to obtain samples of the children's spelling in a short dictation task, and their attempts at retelling, in writing, a story which had been read to them. The same short story was chosen for all classes to make possible comparison between, as well as within, classes. The teachers then spent some time studying, in pairs, the material as a focus for our discussion. Some teachers were disturbed at the limited competence in spelling of some of the older children even on a dictation or spelling test; others were surprised at the competence shown by some of the youngest children in the creative writing situation.

For the five-year-olds a dictated sentence from Marie Clay's book *An Observation Survey of Early Literacy Achievement* (Clay 1993) was used to assess whether the children were yet representing the spoken sounds in their writing. She provides five alternative pairs of sentences which can be used to monitor children's progress and assess the extent to which they are hearing and recording the sounds in words. Thirty-seven sounds are checked in each sentence by counting the child's representation of sounds (phonemes) by letters (graphemes). The sentences I used are scored as follows:

I h a v e   a   b i g   d o g   a t   h o m e.
1 2 3 4   5   6 7 8   9 10 11   12 13   14 15 16

T o d a y I   a m   g o i n g   to t a k e
17 18 19 20   21 22   23 24 25 26 27   28 29 30

h i m   t o   s c h oo l.
31 32 33   34 35 36 37

(Clay 1993, page 68)

One point is scored for each numbered sound (phoneme) which the child has analysed and recorded, giving a total out of 37. Marie Clay stresses that the scoring should be strict, rather than 'liberal'. (See Clay 1993 pages 65–69 for further details of administration, scoring and alternative sentences.)[3]

Some of the children were still producing scribbles, strings of letter-like forms, and could not yet be scored on this task. Examples of different levels of development in response to this task among children within this task who are beginning to write are illustrated below. The attempts at writing the story of these same children are shown in Appendix B. The story is *One Up* by Hazel Townson, which is to be found in full in Appendix B, and

Attempts of five-year-old children to write to dictation.

I ahe d ʊɪ ɡ Teeʒ Tat hom.
2 tP I dm ɡoi

I hemoo diGdog
g ileig to at hour today I am
tler hihto shool

I heve a bag dog at
houme. today I am going
to tok ham to
school

I hasx I have a bag dog at
home. Today I am going to
took ham to SChool

was analysed in Chapter 6 when discussing high frequency words. Examples of seven-year-old children's attempts at retelling this story are to be found in Chapter 10 (see also Appendix B), where the use of stories such as this to help children's written language will be considered.

THE SPELLING WRITING CONNECTION

It is not sufficient that children are able to spell words correctly during a spelling or dictation test. On the other hand they do not necessarily need to be able to spell the words orally. Our aim must be to give them the confidence and skills to be able to spell the key words they need 'on the run' when thinking about something else, namely the content of the message they are attempting to communicate. They may not be able to do this in the early stages, particularly when faced with a complex or creative task. A balance needs to be struck between helping the children towards more conventional ways of representing the words they wish to use in written form, and encouraging them to take risks and use the most appropriate and widest vocabulary they can to meet the purposes for which they are writing. This is one of the values of encouraging even very young children to attempt their own creative writing and spelling. They may be able to read back what they have written, as was the five-year-old whose retelling of 'The Three Little Pigs' is illustrated on page 67. They may be able to write a story collaboratively. A more advanced child could perhaps help as a scribe. In the early stages children may manage to help each other to find errors made in the process of composing, even before they can scan their own work for errors. Beyond a limited number of key words, spelling needs are specific to the task; the words that give problems may differ from person to person. The errors in wrong spelling may also be very different. In one class of seven- and eight-year-olds asked to spell the word 'beautiful' in a spelling test, one of my students found that four children did not attempt it and that there were 21 different wrong spellings from the rest of the class. Most did manage to start the word with a 'b'; however, only two followed with 'e'; 'u' or occasionally 'y' was the second letter! Thus a dictionary would not have been much help with that word for most of these children.[4]

Not only do good spellers by definition make fewer errors, but also the kind of errors they make are likely to be readable as they follow probable patterns in the language. Good spellers tend to know when they are wrong, and the possible alternatives if they are. This enables them on most occasions to check and correct for themselves. For children who have problems with spelling it is important that the focus is on helping them to learn to write accurately, at least the commonest words in English, plus a number of words which they need most frequently when writing at speed, and with minimum attention to the spelling. This requires practice in meaningful tasks.

Even as children come to be able to spell a number of the commonest words, and come to know the most frequent sequences of letters in English words, they may still make errors when engaged in writing; indeed, so do adults, even some who in normal circumstances are good spellers. The more complex the task, the more likely it is that we will make mistakes. I remember discussing his problems with a boy of secondary school age whose spelling was still so insecure that it affected his ability to write fluently, particularly under examination conditions. He explained to me that he could 'see' the words he wanted to spell; his problem, he said, was that he couldn't see them clearly enough! Sadly he had not been given help at a much earlier age and therefore, especially when under stress, he found it difficult to concentrate on the content of what he was writing because his knowledge of the spelling of many words was not automatic enough.

SPELLING: CAUGHT OR TAUGHT

Spelling is 'caught' by some children as they study words while reading. Such children quickly come to observe words within words, common parts of words, groups of letters which appear frequently in English words, and alternative ways of representing the same speech sounds. They therefore move quickly from representing the sounds of spoken words by isolated sounds to attempts at words which at least look like English words. From then they soon begin to spell the commonest words correctly, unless under too much stress in thinking of other things. However, it is easy to be misled in looking at the productions of young able children who have an extensive vocabulary which they are not afraid to use. There may be many spelling errors in their creative work just because of the extensive vocabulary they use.

What is important for all children is that they are helped to move from their own 'creative' spelling towards conventional spelling. This should be done without curbing their desire to produce a variety of written communications, using the most appropriate, richest variety of vocabulary of which they are capable. I still remember with regret my attitude to a small boy in a class of seven-year-olds I taught some years ago. He loved writing stories, the longer the better. He covered pages with them, and could read them back to his enthusiastic class-mates. I am afraid I was more concerned about all the words he spelled wrongly, and less observant than I should have been of the enormous strides he had made, not only in written communication, but also in representation in plausible ways of words in English. One of my colleagues was working with a boy of secondary school age with very severe spelling difficulties. With help this boy was gaining greater confidence in his writing – writing more, using a wider vocabulary and spelling many more of the key words correctly. Unfortunately some of his teachers noticed only the spelling mistakes and assumed he was getting worse! This can happen to young children also.

From an early stage children should be encouraged to scan their work to try and decide which words are correct, which might be wrong and which they are doubtful about. Only then will they know when to ask for help. When assisting children or adults with spelling problems my first aim is to assess just how sensitive they are to their present level of knowledge. I always ask them to bring several examples of their writing and mark it for me themselves, putting a cross above any word they are sure they have wrong, and a question mark above words they are not sure about. This I have found most revealing. Some mark words that are correct; others are doubtful about many; still others have little idea of whether or when they are correct. Children can be encouraged to be self-analytic of their spelling from an early age, and to help others to scan their writing. Discussions with their peers can become valuable learning experiences, the help of the adult being solicited when needed.

It is unfortunate when adults, by their attitude to children's spelling, discourage them from using a wide vocabulary in their written work. Children's spelling errors used to be dismissed as 'mistakes'; more recent studies have shown how children's attempts at spelling can provide information on their developing word knowledge.[5] Children's errors are not accidental; they reflect their knowledge at a particular stage. Children can be helped from their early attempts at their own invented spellings to move towards the conventional spellings of an increasing range of familiar words.

COMMUNICATION IN WRITING

Children have to appreciate that writing is a form of communication; what is written is for reading. From the earliest stages therefore the writing which they are encouraged to produce should be for purposes understood by them. This will include signs, notices, messages and letters as well as short stories. From this they come to appreciate that there are different styles and conventions in writing for different purposes. They must also come to appreciate that what has been written, including the print in books, has been written by someone, that there is an author. If the authors of the different stories and poems they read are identified and discussed, the children will come to realise also that different authors have different styles; some of which they will discover they prefer to others.

To be able to communicate in writing children need to be able to represent the words we speak in written form. For this they need to know:

✦ the letters of the alphabet;

✦ the way to represent sounds on paper;

✦ that spaces are used between words;

✦ how to represent simple regular words;

✦ the probable sequences of letters in English words (this would be different in other languages);

✦ how to write with certainty the commonest words in the language;

✦ when a word is correct and when possibly wrong;

✦ how to find the spelling for words they cannot spell;

✦ how to spell most of the words they need, *when thinking about something else.*

Children whose teachers regard errorless writing as of paramount importance in the early stages may be afraid to take risks in their writing. They may write little or use only a limited vocabulary.

Examples of written work by several seven-year-olds show the quality of language of which some of the children were capable when provided with a stimulating focus, and when encouraged to take risks. Samples of writing from dictation and two rather different tasks were collected from classes of seven-year-olds in five different schools by students who were attending a course of literacy. A short dictation was given so that we could see how adequately each child could spell in that setting; we could then compare their spelling in the more demanding tasks. The children were asked to write a story with the title 'The Last Time it Snowed' (which it had done quite recently). Five examples of the writing this stimulated are shown below; the first three are from children with difficulties. As may be seen, Christopher and Daniel have problems even with spelling. Andrew's writing can be read; however, as a written communication it is very limited. Very different styles of response were stimulated in Philip and Samantha, the extracts from whose writing both show considerable originality.

'The Last Time It Snowed'

Writing by Christopher

The last time it
snowed ther was big
blisuds One day a car sgidd
all the way dowe the Hill
and crash into a Plice car.
and the man was drunk the Plice had
to bya New car.

Writing by Daniel

The Last Time it snowed
Me and My Frand went slaging
and we all was Faell off the
slage and I all was landid in
the hegis. at home me and my
brather made a tanal and a
sum hols in the side for guns.
We made a snow man to throw
snow balls my bruther hit my dad
in the back.

Writing by Andrew

I got up from bed and I
looked outside and it had
snowed so I quickly got washed
and chaned then I jumped
out of the window and when
I landed, the snow was up to
my wast then I called my
brother out and we had
a snow ball fight, then we
built an igloo out of snow
blocks, when we had finnshed
we went inside to lunch.

Extract from writing by Philip

with us. The snow plough had only got
one mile up the lane but we carried
on even though the snow was up to my
waist. were the snow was the shallowist
where it was the deepist it was taller
than mummy. In my welie it was filled
more with snow than with foot.

Extract from writing by Samantha

For the other piece of writing each child was given a wrapped sweet. Discussion with the teacher of a variety of features of the sweets was encouraged as each child examined, unwrapped and finally ate their sweet. The child then wrote about the experience. There were large differences in the writing which was produced, both between children in the same class, and between classes in different schools. In some classes there was a rather stereotyped pattern to the responses to this task; in other classes there was great variety, suggesting that the children were given considerable scope in deciding how to respond.

Three examples are shown, each from a different class (Christopher, Philip and Paul). Christopher, who found even the simple dictation difficult, wrote as follows about the sweet:

it is clue and it is browen it tasst lilok tof

As may be seen, he had problems with all three tasks. Philip had no problems with the dictation. Like most of his class he wrote in the following format:

1. The sweet was round.
2. It smells like orange.
3. We un-rapped it by our ears.
4. It did tased nise.
5. my tased buds did tingle.
6. Inside the hard sweet it was soft.
7. I don't no if it was frait inside the hard sweet.

His writing on the other topic shows confidence both in written language and in spelling as may be seen from the extract on page 131.

The third child, Paul, who also had no problems in the dictation task was much more adventurous in his writing on this topic as may be seen from his writing shown opposite. What did give problems at that stage was the spelling because of the unusual words he used.

These examples illustrate wide differences in the quality of the language, the range of vocabulary used as well as competence in spelling.[6] When we are observing the nature and

E t ing The Sweet

EckSpermenting. Jenefer said it loocked like a dogs face pemSlelthort it Looked Like the top of a moterbike control panull The paper Soundid Like The Sea on the out Side it Was rauff on the in Side of the paper was Stike the Sweet was madeBy needylers Lto Smell Like Lime it was sticke and it tasted like Lime and as hard as rock you have to Suck or fingers it wood get hot if you helled it for a long tim it allso lik took a cake andan old fuSand car wheel and a pot it looked Lime flaeverd Lime flaverd things Vooselle come in green cuLer it allso Looked Like an aming thing in? Uboats it cood be a frisdre

Writing by Paul, aged seven

number of children's spelling errors it is important to consider:

+ the circumstances in which the writing was produced;
+ how important it was to the child;
+ who set the topic;
+ what constraints that placed on the vocabulary which had to be used;
+ how complex the task was for that particular child.

Even a task requiring short answers, with many of the words needed for the answer present in the question can be difficult for some children. As has been shown, the performance of good and poor spellers may differ not only in spelling but in vocabulary, expression and style.

PRACTICAL SUGGESTIONS

Spelling has been considered before other aspects of written language, not because it is regarded as the main ingredient for successful written communication, but because a minimum level of competence is necessary if children's writing is to be meaningful to others. There are ways of ensuring that the foundations of competence in spelling are acquired by young children, and not at the expense of the quality of their written language. Some ideas for use of story as one focus for developing both children's written language and their spelling and punctuation will be reported briefly in the following chapter.

NAME WRITING

Many young children can write at least their first name by the time they start school. Their names have a special significance for them and children should be helped and encouraged to spell them correctly each time they write them. Unfortunately some children have long, rather complicated names. Those who have problems could initially use a shortened form. It would be helpful for them to have a card in front of them with their name on it to which they can refer. However, having checked it letter by letter they should cover the card before attempting to write it, checking their version letter by letter against the model once they have written it. It is important with their names that they see the correct versions repeatedly, and not incorrect versions. It disturbs me to come across children at seven years of age who can still not write their own names with confidence and consistency – admittedly some of the children with problems have names like Christopher, Lawrence or Elizabeth!

Where any child has problems in forming any letters of the alphabet it would be helpful if they have their own individual card to which they can refer, with either all the letters of the alphabet on it, or at least those letters that give problems. It is not always appreciated how much more difficult it is to copy from a distance, especially for children with problems. Where children make a mistake in writing their names, or indeed any other words, it is important that they start again and write the whole word correctly, and do not merely correct the letter or letters which were incorrect. This helps them to gain a picture of the pattern of the whole word.

KEY WORDS

The suggestions made in Chapter 6 for ways of helping children to learn the 100 most frequent words in written English will help not only their reading, but also their spelling. A check could be made of how many of the key words the children can both read and write correctly. It is important that they attempt to write the words in sentences that they think up for themselves; this helps to ensure that they still spell words correctly when thinking of something else (see Appendix A for full list).

WORD STUDY

The children should be encouraged to move from spelling simple phonically regular words to more complex blends. Their interest in word study aroused, they can be helped to spell by studying print and trying to find as many words as possible with similar groupings of letters. They do not always have to be writing the words themselves to come to learn about their properties.[7] One strategy which works well is for a child learning to spell a new word to study it carefully letter by letter, then try and visualise it, trace over it, then write it several times, without looking at the model during the writing, and finally checking for correctness letter by letter. The final step is to make up and write a sentence which includes that word, making sure the key word is still correctly spelled when thinking of something else.

WORD FILES AND WORD BOOKS

Children can be helped to develop their own word books with the words they most often need to spell placed in alphabetic order, initially only by the first letter of the word. This will include a number of the hundred commonest words. When their spelling vocabulary becomes more extensive they will appreciate why it is useful to place the words alphabetically within a section.

When I taught children of primary school age I found it helpful initially to provide each of the children in my class with a box with alphabetic dividers, within which to place their special words; this they found easier initially as they could study one word isolated from the others. They then graduated to word books, and from there to the use of simple dictionaries. The children were given a copy of any word they needed to learn on a slip of paper so that they could put it in their word box, or at a later stage copy into their word book. As I taught a very large class, I found it difficult to individualise the spelling. What was possible was to ensure that all the children knew the most commonly used words and that beyond those, they concentrated on those they needed most, ensuring that those words were so well learned that they would be spelled correctly when needed in meaningful writing. Naturally, some children found spelling easier than others, and some were much slower in learning even the commonest words; some had more limited vocabularies they used in much of their written work; some were just careless! However, with these strategies and a focus only on a very small number of useful words at any one time, all the children made progress, and were enabled to spell a progressively greater number of the words they needed. Only if they spelled incorrectly words they had studied did I express concern; they were encouraged to use as wide a vocabulary as they wished when writing. They could ask for unusual words to be written for them, or if that delayed them or would have spoilt the flow, just take a chance while writing.

It is important that children see words that they use frequently correctly spelled in their own writing, otherwise wrong spelling is being reinforced. For that reason it is preferable that young children use an eraser if they want to change the spelling of a word, rather than score out the wrong word, or put a bracket around it as is sometimes done.

NOTES

1. The following two books provide insights into the understanding of young children which lie behind their early representations of words in written form. Glenda Bissex in her book *GNYS AT WORK: A child learns to write and read* (1980)

traces her son Paul's development in spelling from his earliest attempts, which he was producing before he could read, to his moves towards conventional spelling in a variety of written communications. Charles Read in *Children's Creative Spelling* (1986) analyses the types of representations of words to be found in children's early attempts at writing.

2. During a research project which I directed involving children with learning difficulties in their first year in secondary school, we analysed samples of the pupils' writing in classroom assignments, on a spelling test and on a variety of tasks which we set involving different types of writing and vocabulary. These included writing a scientific report after viewing a video presentation, with the possibility of drafting and redrafting; an explanation for younger children of how to play a game of their choice; descriptive writing based on an experience of their own on the topic 'From Fear to Safety'. We were able to show how strongly the demands of the task influenced the children's choice of vocabulary and apparent spelling competence. The report of the research was entitled *Pupils with Learning Difficulties in the Secondary School: Progress and problems in developing a whole-school policy* (Clark *et al.* 1982). The samples of writing from seven-year-olds referred to in this chapter were collected along similar lines, with tasks designed for the younger age-group. Jennifer Barr who worked with me on the first project devised the tasks for both age groups and used them for her PhD on spelling. A very useful summary of her research for teachers is published in *Understanding Children Spelling* (Barr 1985).

3. Marie Clay in *An Observation Survey of Early Literacy Achievement* (1993) gives guidance on ways of assessing young children's early literacy development; some are given individually to children with difficulties; others are helpful for class use in monitoring the children's progress in the early stages.

4. Margaret Peters was responsible for pioneering research into child and teacher variables which influence children's spelling

progress. *Spelling Caught or Taught?* (Peters 1967) gives practical implications of her work, full details of which are given in *Success in Spelling* (Peters 1970). This contains three graded passages for dictation from one of which the example on page 123 is taken. In that dictation the word 'saucer' appears (as flying saucer), a word which could be read by most eight-year-olds out of context. In her study of about 900 ten-year-olds, about half wrote it correctly; the remainder between them offered around 200 alternative spellings. 'Sauser' was offered by 67 children; about twenty children offered one of the following – sorser, suacer or sacer. The errors of most were such that a dictionary would not have helped them to find the correct spelling.

5. See Note 1.

6. See Note 2.

7. *Learning to Spell: A resource book for teachers* (Todd 1982) gives helpful ideas for the classroom.

STORIES AND THE DEVELOPMENT OF LITERACY

BACKGROUND

In this final chapter, as a way of drawing together ideas which have been mentioned briefly in other chapters, I am adopting a more personal approach, by focusing on the variety of ways in which my students and I have used short stories as a stimulus for young children's reading and writing development. Consideration will be given to how stories can be used to help children with little experience of the language of books in their pre-school or early years in school; young children with limited command of English, spoken or written; and older children who have limited reading ability and have been switched off anything to do with books and writing.

I have chosen the Granada Television series *Time for a Story* as the focus for the discussion in this chapter. The stories for this series were written by well-known children's authors and because Wendy Dewhirst and I were consultants on the series, I have a wealth of illustrative material based on these stories on which I can call.[1] Many other short stories could, I am sure, provide a stimulus in similar ways to those described here. Each story is about 400 to 500 words in length, thus taking about five minutes to read; each is written in the language normally used by that author. Students on a course on literacy which I was teaching at the time the programmes were being arranged had access to the manuscripts of the stories, and found them valuable as a stimulus for practical work with a wide age range of children; later we used the little books published to accompany the series. Over the past ten years I have continued to make use of the more effective stories with children of different ages. The themes, the quality of the language and length of the stories have made them particularly appealing to many children.

With Granada Television's permission I have included the text of two of the stories in Appendix B, *One Up* by Hazel Townson to which reference has already been made in Chapters 6 and 9, and *When the Moon Winked* retold by Sara and Stephen Corrin. I have chosen these two stories as the focus here because of their wide appeal. I showed the television version of the latter story in a school in Singapore committed to the value of stories and books from the earliest stage. The children, who had no access to the materials beyond one viewing of the programme, in return presented me with the most fascinating illustrations, some with 'speech bubbles' as on screen with key dialogue from the king and carpenter; some also made written versions of the story.

More recently, in preparation for a lecture I was giving in Portugal, the teachers who were to attend were invited to read a Portuguese translation of the story to some young children and bring with them to the lecture the written work they produced. This story had appeal to these children also, who after hearing it read to them a couple of times, wrote their own version. Many captured much of the original language; one child was so near to the original that when his version was translated back to English for me, it very closely resembled the authors' version. Another child, only eight years of age, produced a fascinating illustration, showing his grasp not only of the theme of the story but also of many features of astronomy which must have owed much to a study of books; thus showing a rather different aspect of knowledge which can be acquired from books (see opposite).

I have numerous examples of written versions of many of the twenty-eight television stories. Some are from children with very limited ability; others from children who proved capable of outstandingly accurate reporting of both the theme and

An illustration by an eight-year-old, inspired by When the Moon Winked

language. I also have original stories written by quite young children who had prior extensive experience of stories read to them, and therefore were already sensitive to the characteristics both of story and the features of written language. Such children, after hearing one of the series stories, would delight in writing their own story on a similar theme. Two such examples are given here, both by young girls aged around six years. The first child asked if she might write her own story after hearing *Just You Wait* read to her. Her version is shown on page 142 as she wrote it; this can be compared with a typed version of retelling by another child, with only the spelling corrected; from that it is possible to sense both the theme and the language of the original (see page 148).

The second story was stimulated by a story about who should become king of the birds, which challenged another child to write a story about 'Queen of the Reptiles', with appropriate adaptation of the language.

> It was not a happy day for the reptiles because the big ones like the alligotars, the big snakes and the dinosaurs were fighting the little ones like the lizards and turtles They decided to have a competition to find a Queen The reptile

Sally and Priscila.

One day Sally had a nice bouquet and priscila wanted it but Sally said you shall have to wait util you are bigger. The next day sally had a letter to go to the farm at 2pm in the afternoon when priscila came in for tea she saw the letter on the shelf she went to get the letter off the shelf and she road the letter and she went to see Sally I want to go to the farm too be with you said priscila but Sally said No you can not come you might fall in the mud and cut yourself. you will have to wait. On priscila's bithday she had a rocking chair thot was little Sally saw her rocking chair and Said I would like that

Sally had a bouquet

a letter from the farm

But priscila sad No you will have to wait until I am bigger and then I will have a bigger chair.

priscila in her rocking chair

A story written at her own request by a 6½-year-old
after hearing Just You Wait *(read only once)*

who could swim for the longest time would be Qeen So they started to swim lots of reptiles had a rest and only the crocodile was left "I'VE WON! She said – and a little snake came slithering out of her mouth and said "Not so fast I'm not tired and she kept on swimming and she became Queen of the reptiles.

(Spelling and punctuation as in the original)

This child was in a class which had been watching the television series. Her teacher adopted many of the suggestions given on screen and was able to provide a structure for the less confident who might retell the story in a series of pictures, or as they progressed, begin to retell some stories in written form either alone or in groups. Creative opportunities were there too for the more advanced to make up their own stories on similar themes.

ASSESSING WRITTEN LANGUAGE THROUGH STORY

In preparation for a workshop which I conducted in an inner city school (to which brief reference was made in Chapter 9). I arranged for samples of written work from each class to be collected. Each class provided a sample of children's spelling to dictation, or on a spelling test, in addition to their attempts to retell in writing two stories (see Appendix B for examples from a class of five-year-olds). One of the stories they retold was *One Up*, chosen because I felt it would be acceptable to the older as well as the younger children. The staff, working in pairs, were given time to study the samples of written work from which they gained new insights. Such material can bring home the widely different levels of functioning within a single class as well as the potential of some young children. This venture proved particularly interesting in this school since among the samples, were the attempts of children from a class with which I had been working over a period of months – not all now in the same class. Some teachers commented on features of the writing of a number of these children which made them stand out, not only because of their recall of the stories, but also their improved spelling and punctuation. Particularly noted was the use by many of them of appropriate speech marks for the dialogue which they recalled with considerable accuracy.

You also may find this approach useful for within- and across-class comparisons. You might wish also to encourage those children who feel able to do so, to make up their own stories based on a similar theme. This would provide an assessment of another aspect of their development towards literacy, within a framework, yet with scope for creativity.

One of my students undertook a study of seven-year-olds of different levels of ability, all from the same class using the story, *One Up*, which was at that time only in typescript. She read the story twice to the children. They were then encouraged to retell the story to a friend; this retelling was recorded, and analysed to establish how much of the theme and language of the original they had retained in their retelling. They were then asked to retell the story in writing, reassured that it didn't matter if they could not spell the words in the original, but still to use them if they wanted. The language used in the written version was analysed in the same way. This story proved useful because of its episodic structure and ever more exaggerated claims by Tess. It was also short enough for most children to attempt to complete it. The frequently repeated phrase was used by most (even if they couldn't spell some of the words); 'But Charlie could only count up to four, so he changed the subject' as was the twist in the last line: '"I want to learn to count past four," said Charlie.'

Much of the language of the original was retained by most of the children in their retelling, and attempted, even in their written version. There were some children, however, who could recount the story orally in a meaningful way to a friend to whom it was unknown, but were incapable of producing a written version which communicated. Examples of very different levels of writing from these seven-year-olds, all from the same class, are shown opposite and in Appendix B.

Extracts from the retelling of One Up *by four children aged seven.*

I got a new tooth said Charle so
what said Tess Ive got two more
teeth than any body in the world
I bet you haven't said Charle
count them said Tess but Charle
could only count up to four. charlee
changed the subject Ive got new
red boots so what said Tess Ive
got silver ones speicely made
for me because Ive got 12 toes
so Charle changed the subject

tessed I got a hudr biscg
for nofig sed tes wivYoe
dbid seg Crliy Yoe wud bav
fat av a barul Crliy sed
Iv goj a dog as big as a drag
it is a veri big dog it ruv
IIt alfy tes sed I havgot
Ten muciz sed tes havtYoe
Sih The barms on The IIn

chrliy seJ Dgotess Iyv gat to new
Dorl knowtu wr Seqo Choliy she Otors
Dyr got toKnewtiy FF Tess sed to choYiy
Bye choliy eyd owniy upto 4
Choliy serd Iyv got sum Vnew Peobw
Iyv got sun sil veburwts seid Tess seiJto
Chrliy

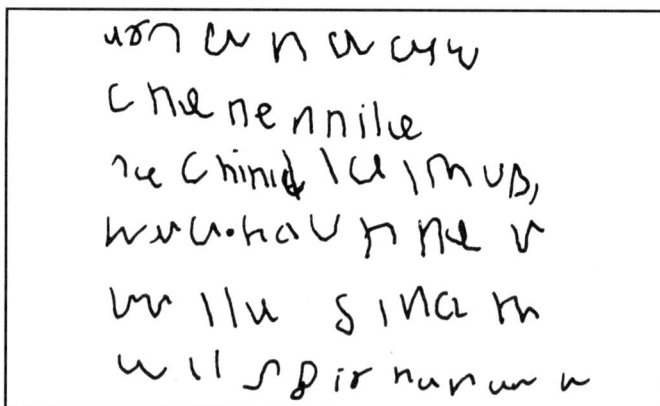

A home visit was paid as part of the project to discuss the children's progress with the parents. Just how concerned most of the parents were about their children's progress became clear, including the parents of the children who were failing. The story had appealed so much to the children, who knew that it was unknown to others, that even the less able had already recounted it at home, that is to a 'real' audience! The parents of the child with the most severe difficulties appealed to the student doing the project to help their daughter. This she did, using the set of stories as the focus. This child became interested not only in written language but in the different styles of the authors and illustrators. Later this student, who was a very experienced teacher, worked with much older children with severe learning difficulties and found these short stories a valuable way into helping very disenchanted teenagers. They were encouraged to write their own short stories for young children on similar themes, using these stories as a framework. This worked well, giving them a structure within which they could produce something approaching coherent written language, some for the first time.

FROM ORAL TO WRITTEN LANGUAGE

Rather than write in generalities about how stories can be used in the classroom, I felt it might be helpful to describe how I used some of these short stories as the focus for work with a class. I worked with a composite class of seven- and eight-year-olds in an inner city school over a period of a few months, during which my visits were never more than weekly. Many of the children had only limited experience of stories; some had little or no reading competence and could spell only a few words correctly with any consistency. In the class there were children from a variety of ethnic backgrounds, for some of whom English was not their mother tongue. After a lecture which I gave in the school, their teacher invited me to work with her. For a few visits I worked only with some of the virtual non-readers in the class, for whom I collected detailed diagnostic information. I soon felt it would be more profitable if I included the whole class in my venture, supporting and encouraging the teacher.

On the basis of an assessment similar to the one described in Chapter 9 (where the children had to write two sentences to dictation and to retell in writing one of the short stories which I read to them); I divided the class into four groups. I used ten of the short stories as the focus for class readings and discussion, including secret voting on favourite stories. This gave an excuse for a brief discussion in which they could all join, to ensure everyone could recall the theme of the stories and the authors.

The two groups which had been able to make an attempt at retelling the first story were encouraged to write their own versions of each of the stories they heard subsequently, and these attempts formed the basis for some of the work we did in their group. As soon as a child had made an attempt at a story which I could read and which approximated to the theme, I typed the version. It was interesting to see how close to the language of the original the children were able to keep, including the more unusual phrases and vocabulary. A few, whose mother tongue was not English, omitted the article on occasion. For the typed version the spelling was corrected and punctuation was inserted, including the speech marks which were important in most of these stories. However, I made only essential corrections, putting brackets round anything I changed, which was never more than the insertion or deletion of one or two words. The children then had the excitement of seeing their versions typed, with the title and retold by.... It was then possible to base some of the work in the groups on these typed versions.

The typed version of one story by a child for whom English is his second language is shown below:

> *Just You Wait* retold by...
>
> Robert had a kite with a dragon on the head.
>
> Brian said, "I want one like that."
>
> Robert said, "If there was a big wind the wind will blow you away. We might not see you again. You will have to wait."
>
> Robert had a knife with lots of things on it, like can openers.
>
> "I want one like that."
>
> "If you had a knife like (that) you might cut your fingers off. You will have to wait."
>
> Robert had roller skates. He can jump over buckets and keep rolling on the other side.
>
> "I want a pair of roller skates."
>
> "If you had a pair of roller skates you might fall over and bump your head and if you try to jump over buckets you might break   ."
>
> On Brian's birthday he got a wigwam. Brian crept in.
>
> Robert said, "Can I come in?"
>
> Brian said, "If you come in you might get stuck in the middle. They might have to pull your legs off. You'll have to wait. When I'm bigger I am going to get a bigger wigwam. You might fit in it."

I have changed none of what he wrote, and the only word he omitted, 'that', I inserted in brackets. As can be seen he had captured the theme and the 'feel' of some of the language. It would not have been helpful, however, for him at this stage to have worked with, or on his version as it had so many spelling mistakes, many changes and incorrect punctuation. I could guess the words intended because I knew the story.

The two more advanced groups worked in pairs discussing incidents or expressions either had omitted and how necessary these were. They could insert these on the typed versions. They also learned how speech marks work, by highlighting on the typed versions in different colours the words said by different characters, such as Brian and Robert in the example above. Soon they began to use these in their own writing. I only typed a few stories for each child, then they were on their own, more sensitive to their own errors, or at least to those of their partners. The original stories were all made available on audio tape read by their teacher, so that the children could listen as often as they wanted to their favourite stories at the listening centre. Some children, either alone or in pairs, decided to make me their own versions of the stories, with illustrations; their teacher encouraged this and the idea spread. I was given presents of several well-illustrated little books (see below for an extract from one based on *When the Moon Winked* by another child for whom English was a second language). My attempts to get these children to write their own stories on similar themes were initially relatively unsuccessful. Their attempts collapsed into rather limited, often ungrammatical spoken language, as

Extract from a book retelling of **When the Moon Winked** *(see Appendix B for complete version).*

2. He
to build
called
him
his
a
carpenter
tower.

3. The
do
a
carpenter
plan.
pretended
to

wheres my
tower.
If you don
build that
tower
in three
days you
look out

seen in the writing of many older backward readers. This showed their continuing need for the support of orally presented written language.

After seeing their attempts at the first story, *Just You Wait*, I did not allow the two groups with the greatest difficulties to write the other stories for me, and the reason for this was explained to them; until they could spell more of the common words I wouldn't be able to guess what they meant and therefore would be unable to type their versions accurately. This, their teacher reported, proved a real incentive to improve! Meanwhile they provided front covers and illustrations for the class books of retold stories. Some of the illustrations had speech bubbles with dialogue, or an extract from the story; for these they were given a model to copy if needed, 'to ensure our books didn't have errors!' The illustrations shown on page 152 are from two of the children with little or no reading competence. Many alternative activities were devised for these children to improve their ability to read and write the key words (along the lines suggested in Chapter 6) and to improve their understanding of the patterns of written English (as discussed in Chapter 7). Throughout the following weeks they also enjoyed the experience of listening to written language read and reread in the classroom. As a stimulus for their first attempt at writing they were read one of the stories, which was also made available to them on tape; they were encouraged to keep this secret from the other half of the class. They then produced their written versions for a book, which if they were beginning to communicate with the reader, were typed for them.

The progress made by the children in this class owed much to the enthusiastic support of the teacher who followed up the activities I undertook on my relatively infrequent visits. I had the advantage of being a visitor who introduced novel ideas and brought new materials, who also was able to withdraw the children in smaller groups of about eight, even if for only short periods, which they all enjoyed. My intervention on its own could have had little prolonged effect on the children's progress.

*Two examples of illustrations for the class books of
retold stories by children with little reading competence*

Tortoises Tug-of-war

Just You Wait

What it did do, with the support of the teacher, was give
renewed hope to some of the children who must inevitably have
been coming to regard themselves as failures, and new
challenges to the more able.

THE FOUNDATIONS OF CREATIVITY

Imitation can be a valuable foundation for creativity. I have
many examples of stories written by quite young children who
have had extensive experience of stories read to them at home

and in the classroom. Initially they may follow the theme of a single story they have heard, as did the two six-year-olds whose original stories are illustrated on pages 141–143. When children use a story they have heard, or read, as a model they are still being creative – indeed one of the stories cited here, *When the Moon Winked*, is itself not original in theme. Children as they become more confident and widen their experience may come to use vocabulary and expressions from a variety of authors and themes, which while enriched by the books they have read, owe much to their own experiences.

LITERACY AND COMPUTERS

Young children have many problems to overcome in their early attempts to communicate in writing. They have to decide what to write and how to represent their thoughts so that someone else can read them. They also face a further difficulty as a consequence of their limited motor co-ordination. Their need to concentrate on the act of writing may interfere with their 'composition' and they may be unable to show just how much they are capable of communicating in written language. The advent of computers, and in particular word processors, provides a new technology which can be of great help to children in their writing. Computers enable them to see an accurate representation of the letters; they can erase any errors and add punctuation without the effort of rewriting. Not least they are able to redraft their attempts, improving the language, either on their own or in discussion with others.

When word processors were first introduced into primary classrooms they were in short supply, and few classrooms had access to a printer. Now that equipment is much more available children can produce their own typed versions of their work, with the language improved, and errors eliminated in the final version in a way that would put intolerable stress on them were they to attempt to produce a handwritten fair copy. This could form a valuable support to, or development from, the kind of activities described in this chapter.

In Chapter 8 an example was given of children using a recent computer program to assist them in the early stages of learning to read. A very different way in which computer programs can be used to great effect is in helping children to appreciate the structure of written English and the pattern of letters within words. I still retain a vivid memory of a visit I paid to a primary school in The West Midlands in the early 1980s when software for primary schools was still relatively rare. There was a word processor in the school, but no printer available to the children. The headteacher had a group of children aged about eight years of age grouped round the computer where they were engaged in a lively, focused discussion as they attempted to reveal the text hidden on screen. The package was flexible and enabled the teacher to type in passages of his choice, which could be very familiar or unknown, prose or poetry. He could reveal as little or much of the text initially as he wished; that is, punctuation only, the initial letters of words, dashes for letters, or spaces between words. A request could be made for particular words or letters to be revealed, the aim being to discover the hidden passage in as few moves as possible. More or less elaborate scoring systems could be used. The creative learning experience for those children arose from a combination of the novelty of the computer, the nature of the software and the way that the teacher planned and implemented its use. He made it possible for all the children in the class to have experience of what was, at that time, a scarce resource, at levels and in ways which met their needs. He provided them with both a stimulus for discussion and insights into the nature of written language.[2]

It is all too easy for computers to be seen as a learning resource in the classroom, or solution for children with problems, without clear objectives being planned as to precisely how they will facilitate the children's learning. Software packages advertised as aids to reading, writing or spelling are no less likely to become merely time fillers than other commercial materials advertised as aids to literacy merely because they may be more sophisticated. They must be as critically evaluated as any other commercially produced product.

NOTES

1. The Granada Television series for schools, *Time for a Story*, referred to here involved 28 ten minute programmes. During each programme one of the stories was read once while illustrations and selected print from the story were shown on screen. Depending on the theme there was a brief introduction or time after the reading to re-present the story with the key phrases retained, but told through pictures, or with the children joining in some of the dialogue. Teachers' booklets were available with suggestions for further activities based on each story and titles of stories on a similar theme. The stories were produced as individual little books which could be purchased together with an associated audio tape. Unfortunately, the television programmes and teachers' booklets are no longer available. See Appendix B for the full text and information about two of the stories together with examples of children's retelling of the stories.

2. At a conference on *Reading and the New Technologies* in 1984 Jonathan Anderson gave a paper in which he discussed the use in Australia of programs similar to the one referred to in this chapter. To quote:

> Much learning about language generally results – for example, learning about the probabilities of occurrence of letters singly, of diagraphs and, as the text is progressively displayed, of phrases and of words. It is not an easy task, so be warned. Nevertheless, the game format of buying letters of the alphabet, working in groups, making hypotheses, to have these confirmed or rejected as the text is slowly revealed, is quite an enjoyable experience.
>
> (J. Anderson, 1985, 'Reading, writing and learning with microcomputers' from *Reading and the New Technologies* edited by J. Ewing, pages 104–105)

AFTERWORD: THE WAY AHEAD

Clearly some form of national curriculum is here to stay in Britain, as in many other countries, with greater central control of the subjects taught. Some form of national testing is also likely to continue, whether through teacher assessment in the early stages or by nationally imposed tests. It is to be hoped that within the national curriculum as it is now developing children will be able to experience a variety of creative learning experiences in school, with continuity, breadth and balance in their education. It is to be hoped that any move to 'the basics' is not 'Back to Basics' if by that we risk ignoring the insights which can be drawn from research.

As has been shown here most young children in a print-filled environment such as ours, enter school already actively seeking to gain an understanding of the meaning of print, forming and testing hypotheses. Their homes have already contributed a great deal to the outlook children bring to school and to the range of understanding of literacy-related activities which they have acquired. Parents and the community will continue to exert a powerful influence on children's attitudes to literacy which schools will ignore at their peril. What is clear is that children learn at very different speeds and in very different ways; not always what the teacher is teaching. There is no magic formula whereby all children will learn to read and write.

The foundations of literacy, and attitudes towards it, are laid for most adults in the early years. If we are to meet the needs of young children we must not only learn about, but from them, listening to and observing them. If we are to be effective we must learn to work in partnership with the parents, listening to and learning from them, as well as supporting them. Only then will schools provide a learning environment which encourages children, enabling them to become literate, and to gain satisfaction and enjoyment from spoken and written language.

HIGH FREQUENCY WORDS

McNally and Murray prepared a list of key words common in most written English. Although this list was originally drawn up in the early 1960s it is still in current use and can be obtained from Ladybird. It is contained in *Read with Me: Key words to reading, a parent/teacher guide* (Murray and Corby 1990). A full discussion of its relevance to reading and writing is to be found in Chapter 6.

The following 100 key words account for about half the total words in everyday reading material. A further 100 words only account for 10–15 per cent more of the words; beyond this there is little added advantage for each additional 100 words.

The following 12 words account for about 25 per cent of the total words:

> a and he I in is it of that the to was

The following 20 words account for a further 10 per cent of the total words:

> all as at be but are for had have him
>
> his not on one said so they we with you

The following 68 words account for another 20 per cent of the total words:

> about an back been before big by call came can come
>
> could did do down first from get go has her here if into
>
> just like little look made make me more much must
>
> my no new now off old only or our other out over right
>
> see she some their them then there this two when up
>
> want well went were what where which who will your

This word count concerns the proportion of the *total* number of words. A study of the number of *different* words shows just how many of such words appear relatively infrequently; yet speedy recognition of these is also crucial for meaningful reading (see Chapter 7).

N.B. Even within the commonest 200 words there are few nouns: these are more likely to be influenced by the topic.

The full text of two of the short stories discussed in Chapters 6 and 10 is given in the following pages. Permission has been given by Granada Television for teachers to copy them to enable full use to be made of the ideas suggested in this book. These stories are two of the twenty-eight stories specially written by well-known children's authors for a television series for schools entitled *Time for a Story* for which Wendy Dewhirst and I were educational consultants.

ONE UP BY HAZEL TOWNSON

One Up by Hazel Townson was analysed in full in Chapter 6. This story does not need any introduction, before the first reading. The children will quickly get the message about the different characters of Charlie and Tess and the pattern whereby the same expression appears at the end of each episode.

> 'But Charlie could only count up to four,
>
> so he changed the subject.'

This line appears in the retelling of this story by most children. There are five main episodes in the story which the children could be encouraged to include in their drawings and writing. The order of the episodes is crucial as each boast by Tess becomes more extravagant. Younger children may need help to think up episodes which vary in the extravagance of the claim if developing their own stories.

One young child who had listened to the story on her own was to retell it to a friend who had not heard it. She was overheard reassuring her friend that she would enjoy the story, that there was a little boy Charlie and a girl Tess, who was awful! She had got the message.

Shown after the story are retellings by four five-year-olds (whose attempts at dictation are shown on pages 124 and 125) and a seven-year-old (an extract from which is shown on page 145).

ONE UP
BY HAZEL TOWNSON

"I've got a new tooth," Charlie said.
"I've got two new teeth," said Tess.
"I've got two teeth more than anybody else in the world."
"I'll bet you haven't," Charlie said.
"Yes, I have, then! Look, you can count them if you like!"
Tess opened her mouth very wide.
But Charlie could only count up to four,
so he changed the subject.

"I've got new red wellies," said Charlie.
"I've got new silver wellies," said Tess.
"They have to be specially made because of my extra toes.
I've got twelve toes – six on each foot."
"You can't have!" Charlie said.
"You just count them!" Tess was already pulling off her socks.
But Charlie could only count up to four,
so he changed the subject.

"My mum gave me a slice of apple pie," said Charlie,
"for tidying my room."
"That's nothing!" said Tess.
"My mum gave me a hundred biscuits
for not doing anything."
"If you ate a hundred biscuits you'd be as fat as a barrel,"
said Charlie.
"You come to tea at our house and I'll show you," said Tess.
"I'll eat a hundred biscuits as easy as winking.
And a hundred plates of jelly and cream as well."
But Charlie knew that when Tess had eaten four biscuits
he would lose count.
Anyone could eat four biscuits at a time,
even Charlie.
But Charlie could only count up to four,
so he changed the subject.

"Our dog sleeps under my bed," said Charlie.

"He's as big as a dragon."

"So what?" said Tess.

"My ten pet monkeys sleep *in* my bed with me.

They have a nice, comfy night.

Your dog isn't comfy on the floor.

The floor's hard and dusty and cold."

"Our dog likes it best under my bed," said Charlie.

"And our dog's real. Our dog can growl like a lion.

Your monkeys are only toys,

or your mum wouldn't let them sleep in your bed."

"My monkeys ARE real.

They wear real pyjamas, so there!" said Tess

"Haven't you seen their pyjamas

hanging on the washing line?"

"I've seen *your* pyjamas," said Charlie.

"I don't wear ten lots of pyjamas at once," said Tess.

"Come round to our house next washing day, then you'll see.

You'll be able to count them.

Two yellow lots, two pink, two blue, two green

and two purple. *My* pyjamas are white."

But Charlie could only count up to four,

so he changed the subject.

"I'm going to the circus tomorrow," said Charlie,

"So I can't come to your house anyway."

"Oh, we're always going to the circus," said Tess.

"We've been lots of times already this week."

She began counting on her fingers.

"Twice on Monday, once on Tuesday, three times on Wednesday,

and we're going again on Saturday afternoon.

It gets very boring."

When Tess had gone home, Charlie said to his mother:

"I don't want to play with Tess tomorrow."

"What do you want to do then, tomorrow?"

"I want to learn how to count past four," said Charlie.

Attempts by five-year-olds to write the story One Up.

I hff 2 tnn

I hff I tnn

I hff nnt Bnss
I att u ones Bisi
mom om

I go to urert tsow taust It
be2bd ye hsbeh saw bsse
tstsy ye
foro I ye urert to saw
I y saw taus E I
saw o rort cat Twret qu to 4
saw taus E bestsy

chll said I heve 2 naw
taqs I baat yuu hwoat
suld tousI have 2 tqqs toun
ifr rw Look yuu will cct
them bat chll ulb cuot to
4 sqas he cuoeed the
sbect

I have two New tnth I have
three New tnth I have niheteen
New tnth caet men·

A seven-year-old retells the story One Up.

I got a new tooth Said Charle So
what said Tess Ive got two more
teeth than any body in the world
I bet you havent said Charle
count them Said Tess but charle
could only count up to four charlee
changed the subject Ive got new
red boots so what Said Tess Ive
got silver ones speicely made
for me because Ive got 12 toes
So Charle changed the subject
Ive got a dog as big as dragon
and he growls like a lion
Ive got ten monkegs they sleep
in my bed yoar dogs not
comfey under your bed
your monkegs are toy monkey there not
Said Tess they were real Pyjamers
Two pink Two yellow and Purple
and green. so charle changed the
subject Ivne going to the Circas
tommorow so what said Tess Ive been
twice On mon day once on Tuesday
and Im going on satueday
after nooo charle said to his
mother I don't want Play with
Tess tomorow I want to lern
over four

WHEN THE MOON WINKED BY SARA AND STEPHEN CORRIN

The second story, *When the Moon Winked* retold by Sara and Stephen Corrin was referred to briefly in Chapters 6 and 10. This story readily lends itself to be retold in the form of a series of pictures and there follows two examples of ways in which young children have created their own illustrated versions. The version on page 166 is by a child whose mother tongue is not English (an extract is shown on pages 149 and 150). The version on page 167 is a collaborative venture by two children with very limited reading competence.

Before reading this story in the class it would be helpful to check that the children understand what 'to wink' means, and that we sometimes wink when we share a joke. They could try winking with one eye or the other.

After you have read the story once to the children, you might like to put some of the King's dialogue on cards to be held up at the appropriate time, or on the blackboard so that on a second reading the children can join in with the King's words. The dialogue by the King is also easily remembered by the children.

This story could be followed by other stories developed by the children with a similar theme such as

+ The Queen who wanted to touch the bottom of the ocean;
+ The Elephant who wanted to catch the wind;
+ The Mouse who wanted to fly.

WHEN THE MOON WINKED
RETOLD BY SARA AND STEPHEN CORRIN

Once there was a King who wanted to touch the moon.
This was the ONLY thing he could think of,
day and night, day and night.
He even dreamt about it.
"I must, I must, I REALLY must touch the moon,"
he kept muttering.

He called his Head Carpenter to him.
"I've simply got to touch that moon," he told him,
"and your job will be to build me a tower
that will reach up to the sky."
The carpenter was scared.
He dare not tell the King that such a tower was impossible.
He would have to build it somehow – with wood, of course.
But even if every tree were cut down
there still wouldn't be enough wood.
So he pretended to be making plans.

The King grew impatient.
"Where's my tower?" he roared.
"I'll give you three days," he told the carpenter,
"and if it's not ready by then, look out!"
The carpenter was now beginning to panic.
"Tell you what," his wife said to him, "ask the King to order
everyone to bring every box they have to the palace."

So the King commanded everybody
to bring all their boxes to the palace grounds.
Then the Head Carpenter got them
to pile the boxes one on top of the other to the very last box.
"Not half high enough!" shrieked the King.
"Have all the trees in my kingdom
chopped down to make more boxes."

Then the new boxes were piled on top of the others.
It was now a very high tower indeed.
"Let me try it first to make sure it's safe,"
said the Head Carpenter.
"Oh no, you won't!" roared the King.
"I'm the one who's going to touch the moon."

The King started to climb.
He climbed and he climbed and he climbed, got to the top
and stretched out his hand.
Ah! He still couldn't quite touch it!
"One more box," he shouted down, "one more box."
But there wasn't a single box to be found.
Not a scrap of wood anywhere to make one.
Every single tree had been felled.

The King was LIVID!
So near and yet so far, he thought.
Then he had a brainwave (or so he imagined).
"Get the bottom box of the tower," he ordered,
"and fetch it up here to me."
"You mean the... the bottom one?" gasped the carpenter.
"Yes," roared the King, "and quick about it
or you'll be in trouble!"

The Head Carpenter was certain he saw the moon give a wink.
Very, very carefully he pulled out the bottom box...
AND WHAT TO YOU THINK HAPPENED?

From somewhere underneath the hundreds and hundreds
and hundreds of boxes, out crawled the King,
his face all red and sheepish.
His courtiers hurriedly hustled him back to his palace.

Do you think the King
ever again tried to touch the moon?

A young child's book based on When the Moon Winked

1. Once there was a King who wanted to touch the moon.

"I must I must I really must touch the moon"

2. He called his carpenter to build him a tower.

3. The carpenter pretended to do a plan.

"Wheres my tower"

"If you dont build that tower in three days you look out"

4. The king said "I must I must I really must touch the moon.

"I must I must I really must touch the moon"

5. The carpenter's wife said she had a plan she tell the King to get every box.

6. The carpenter said "I will climd if it is fisrt ok" and see if it

"no Im the one who's going to climd it

6. So the King climd it he climd it but he still did not touch it. The moon winked.

"one more box get one the botten"

7. The carpenter pulled the botten box and all the boxes fell down

The King never wanted to touch the moon.

Another example of a book written and illustrated
after hearing When the Moon Winked

When the moon Winked

The King wanted to touch the moon

So he asked the carpeter to get lots of boxes.

So the carpeter got lots of boxes

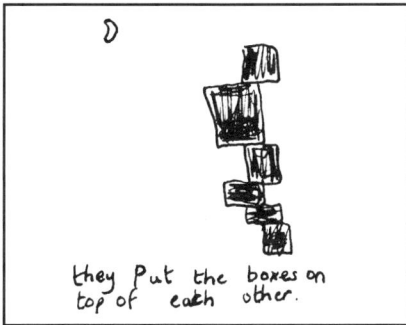

they put the boxes on top of each other.

then the king climbed up it.

but he needed one more box then the moon Winked

so the carpeter got the bottom box and they all fell down

REFERENCES

This is a full list of all sources cited in the book. Some of the earlier publications may now be available only from libraries. Where I am aware of a later edition I have noted this. Publications which have further information relevant to a particular chapter are referred to in notes at the end of the chapter; fuller information is given here.

Adams, M.J. (1990a) *Beginning to Read: Thinking and learning about print*, The MIT Press.

Adams, M.J. (1990b) *Beginning to Read: The new phonics in context*, Heinemann. (This is a summary of the book above.)

Anderson, J. (1985) 'Reading, writing and learning with microcomputers', from Ewing, J. (Ed.) *Reading and the New Technologies*, Heinemann Educational Books for UKRA.

Balmuth, M. (1982) *The Roots of Phonics: A historical introduction*, McGraw-Hill.

Barr, J.E. (1985) *Understanding Children Spelling*, Scottish Council for Research in Education.

Barrett, G. (1986) *Starting School: An evaluation of the experience*, Centre for Applied Research in Education, University of East Anglia.

Beard, R. (Ed.) (1993) *Teaching Literacy: Balancing perspectives*, Hodder & Stoughton.

Bennett, N. and Kell, J. (1989) *A Good Start? Four year olds in infant schools*, Blackwell Education.

Bentley, D., Karavis, S. and Reid, D. (1990) *The Child, the Teacher and the National Curriculum Key Stage 1 English*, The Reading and Language Information Centre, University of Reading.

Beverton, S., Hunter-Carsch, M., Obrist, C. and Stuart, A. (1993) *Running Family Reading Groups*, United Kingdom Reading Association.

Bissex, G.L. (1980) *GNYS AT WRK: A child learns to write and read*, Harvard University Press.

Bradley, L. and Bryant, P. (1985) *Rhyme and Reason in Reading and Spelling*, University of Michigan Press.

Butler, D. (1979) *Cushla and her Books*, Hodder & Stoughton. (New edition without the illustrations published in 1987 by Penguin.)

Butler, D. and Clay, M. (1987) *Reading Begins at Home: Preparing children for reading before they go to school*, Heinemann.

Carroll, L. (1939) *Lewis Carroll: The complete works*, The Nonesuch Library.

Chall, J.S. (1967) *Learning to Read: The great debate*, McGraw-Hill.

Chall, J.S. (1979) 'The great debate: ten years later, with a modest proposal for reading stages', from Resnick, L. and Weaver, P. (Eds.) *Theory and Practice of Early Reading*, Lawrence Erlbaum.

Clark, M.M. (1970) *Reading Difficulties in Schools*, Penguin Education. (New edition published in 1979 by Heinemann Educational.)

Clark, M.M. (1976) *Young Fluent Readers: What can they teach us?* Heinemann Educational.

Clark, M.M. (1989) *Understanding Research in Early Education*, Gordon and Breach.

Clark, M.M., Barr, J. and McKee, F. (1982) *Pupils with Learning Difficulties in the Secondary School: Progress and problems in developing a whole-school policy*, available from The Scottish Council for Research in Education.

Clay, M.M. (1972) *Reading: the Patterning of Complex Behaviour*, Heinemann Educational. (A new edition of this was published in 1991.)

Clay, M. (1987) *Writing Begins at Home: Preparing children for writing before they go to school*, Heinemann.

Clay, M.M. (1991) *Becoming Literate: The construction of inner control*, Heinemann.

Clay, M.M. (1993) *An Observation Survey of Early Literacy Achievement*, Heinemann.

Department of Education and Science (1975) *A Language for Life* (The Bullock Report), HMSO.

Department of Education and Science (1988a) *Report of the Inquiry into the Teaching of English Language* (The Kingman Report), HMSO.

Department of Education and Science (1988b) *English for ages 5 to 11* (The Cox Report), HMSO.

Donachy, W. (1979) 'Parental participation in preschool education', from Clark, M.M. and Cheyne, W.M. (Eds.) *Studies in Preschool Education*, Hodder & Stoughton.

Donaldson, M. (1978) *Children's Minds*, Fontana/Collins.

Donaldson, M. and Reid, J. (1985) 'Language skills and reading: a developmental perspective', from Clark, M.M. (Ed.) *New Directions in the Study of Reading*, Falmer Press.

Ferreiro, E. and Teberosky, A. (1982) *Literacy Before Schooling*, Heinemann Educational.

Fox, C. (1992) 'Stories and the literacy environment of the classroom', from Harrison, C. and Coles, M. (Eds.) *The Reading for Real Handbook*, Routledge.

Goelman, H., Oberg, A. and Smith, F. (Eds.) (1984) *Awakening to Literacy*, Heinemann Educational.

Goodacre, E.J. (1974) *Hearing Children Read: Including a list of reading schemes and other materials*, Centre for the Teaching of Reading, University of Reading.

Goswami, U. (1994) 'The role of analogies in reading development', *Support for Learning*, 9, 1, 22–26.

Goswami, U. and Bryant, P. (1990) *Phonological Skills and Learning to Read*, Lawrence Erlbaum.

Harrison, C. and Coles, M. (Eds.) (1992) *The Reading for Real Handbook*, Routledge.

Heath, S.B. (1983) *Ways with Words: Language, life and work in communities and classrooms*, Cambridge University Press.

Holdaway, D. (1979) *The Foundations of Literacy*, Ashton Scholastic.

House of Commons, Education, Science and Arts Committee (1991) *Standards of Reading in Primary Schools*, Vol. 1 Report, Vol. 2 Minutes of evidence and appendices, HMSO.

Kennedy, A. (1984) *The Psychology of Reading*, Methuen.

Lane, M. (1991) 'Surveying all the factors: reading research', *Language and Learning*, 6, 8-13.

Lomax, C.M. (1979) 'Implications – the assessment of young children', from Clark, M.M. and Cheyne, W.M. (Eds.) *Studies in Preschool Education*, Hodder & Stoughton.

McNally, J. and Murray, W. (1968) *Key Words to Literacy and the Teaching of Reading*, Schoolmaster Publishing Company.

Medwell, J. (1994) 'Using the Sherston naughty stories', *Language and Literacy News*, UKRA, 13, 4–5.

Minns, H. (1990) *Read it to Me Now! Learning at home and at school*, Virago.

Moon, C. (1993) *Individualised Reading: A teacher guide to readability levels at Key Stages 1 and 2*, Reading and Language Information Centre, University of Reading.

Murray, W. and Corby, J. (1990) *Read with Me! Key words to reading. A parent teacher guide*, Ladybird.

Payton, S. (1984) *Developing Awareness of Print*, Off-set Publication No. 2 Educational Review, University of Birmingham.

Perera, K. (1993) 'The "good book": Linguistic aspects', from Beard, R. (Ed.) *Teaching Literacy: Balancing perspectives*, Hodder & Stoughton.

Peters, M.L. (1967) *Spelling Caught or Taught?* Routledge and Kegan Paul. (New edition 1985.)

Peters, M.L. (1970) *Success in Spelling* Cambridge Institute of Education.

Phinn, G. (1992) 'Choosing books for young readers: habituated to the vast', from Harrison, C. and Coles, M. (Eds.) *The Reading for Real Handbook*, Routledge.

Read, C. (1986) *Children's Creative Spelling*, Routledge and Kegan Paul.

Ross, T. (1985) *Oscar Buys the Biscuits*, Granada Television.

Sinclair, J. (Ed.) (1987) *Collins Cobuild English Language Dictionary*, Collins.

Smith, F. (1971) *Understanding Reading: A psycholinguistic analysis of reading and learning to read*, Holt, Rinehart and Winston. (Over the years several revised editions have been published.)

Southgate, V. and Roberts, G.R. (1970) *Reading – Which Approach?* Hodder & Stoughton.

Suffolk County Council (1993a) *Rhyme: A resource for teachers of reading*, Suffolk County Council.

Suffolk County Council (1993b) *Sounds Interesting: Practical ideas for developing phonics in the classroom*, Suffolk County Council.

Teale, W.H. (1984) 'Reading to young children: its significance for literacy development', from Goelman, H., Oberg, A. and Smith, F. (Eds.)

Awakening to Literacy, Heinemann Educational.

Tizard, B. and Hughes, M. (1984) *Young Children Learning: Talking and thinking at home and at school*, Fontana.

Tizard, B., Blatchford, P., Burke, J., Farquhar, C. and Plewis, I. (1988) *Young Children at School in the Inner City*, Lawrence Erlbaum.

Todd, J. (1982) *Learning to Spell: A resource book for teachers*, Basil Blackwell.

Tough, J. (1977) *The Development of Meaning: A study of children's use of language*, Allen and Unwin.

Van Lierop, M. (1985) 'Predisposing factors in early literacy: A case study', from Clark, M.M. (Ed.) *New Directions in the Study of Reading*, Falmer Press.

Wells, G. (1986) *The Meaning Makers: Children learning language and using language to learn*, Heinemann.

Wray, D., Lewis, M. and Cox, C. (1994) 'Young researchers at work', *Language and Literacy News*, UKRA, 13, 4–5.

INDEX